Democracy Inside

D1562490

Democracy Inside

Participatory Innovation in
Unlikely Places

ALBERT W. DZUR

OXFORD
UNIVERSITY PRESS

OXFORD
UNIVERSITY PRESS

Oxford University Press is a department of the University of Oxford. It furthers
the University's objective of excellence in research, scholarship, and education
by publishing worldwide. Oxford is a registered trade mark of Oxford University
Press in the UK and certain other countries.

Published in the United States of America by Oxford University Press
198 Madison Avenue, New York, NY 10016, United States of America.

Library of Congress Cataloging-in-Publication Data
Names: Dzur, Albert W., author.
Title: Democracy inside : participatory innovation in unlikely places /
Albert W. Dzur.
Description: New York, NY, United States of America : Oxford University
Press, [2018] | Includes bibliographical references.
Identifiers: LCCN 2018009284 | ISBN 978-0-19-065866-3 (hard cover) |
ISBN 978-0-19-065867-0 (pbk.) | ISBN 978-0-19-065868-7 (updf) |
ISBN 978-0-19-065869-4 (epub)
Subjects: LCSH: Group decision making. | Political participation. |
Democracy. | Democracy and education. | Education and state—Decision
making. | Education and state—Citizen participation. | Restorative
justice—Decision making. | Restorative justice—Citizen participation. |
Municipal government—Decision making. | Municipal government—Citizen
participation.
Classification: LCC HM746.D98 2018 | DDC 302.3—dc23
LC record available at https://lccn.loc.gov/2018009284

1 3 5 7 9 8 6 4 2

Paperback printed by Webcom Inc., Canada
Hardback printed by Bridgeport National Bindery, Inc., United States of America

For Kiran and Neena

Contents

Preface

*And now, methinks, this wider wood-path is not bad, for it
admits of society more conveniently. Two can walk side by
side in it in the ruts, aye, and one more in the horse-track.*
—HENRY DAVID THOREAU

Trails

It is hard to see the forest path in the fall just after the leaves come down,
blown by cool winds. It is hard to see in winter on days when there is enough
snow. It is hard to see, too, in early spring with the new grass and also after a
summer storm washes mud and sand around. I know it is there, though, and
I find it every time by moving along.

Democracy is hard to see sometimes too. It keeps getting covered up and
we keep having to find it, together. It is in how we work, and talk, and live,
though, as this book will show. Is it part of our nature? No. Is it everywhere
the same? No. Does it make everything it touches better? No. Democracy
is simply the sharing of power to handle collective problems. It takes many
forms and can be both efficacious and fraught with compromise or indeci-
sion. At the moment, though, we seem to have lost hope in its possibilities;
we are not able to find the path.

I want us to get a better grip on democracy, as a concept, because we often
set either too low or too high a standard. In some high school and college
government textbooks, democracy is achieved merely by following the rules,
obeying the law, and showing up to vote (when we feel strongly enough, that
is). In other, more philosophical conversations, democracy is attained only
when certain cognitive, deliberative, or distributive demands are met that protect decision-making forums from public ignorance, strategic bargaining, and

resource inequalities. By contrast, I want to bring things down to earth: to specific places, routines, and above all to specific people in proximity to one another sharing tasks, information, and decisions. Democracy means sharing power to shape a common public life with others who are not the same as us. This is more demanding than rule-following, obedience, and voting, but it also differs from the philosophers' standards.

Consent, legitimacy, sovereignty, and myriad other terms used in political theory can sound legalistic and formal, as if democracy were only about laws, regulations, and voting rules. Instead of the legal, regulative, and electoral, however, I want to stress the productive as being the vital core of democracy: we share tasks that constitute us as a reflective and democratic people—we produce education, justice, security, and more.[1] We learn how to do this task-sharing productive activity well or poorly, consciously or not, in schools, workplaces, street corners, hospitals, courtrooms, and many other places. Cognition does not drive democratic work in democratic places; it follows it. Laws and rules help shape institutions that allow citizens to act, of course, but it is the action itself that makes them democratic.

Pessimism and abstraction pervade contemporary thinking about democracy, as we will discuss in Chapter 1. In academia, some worry about "oligarchic" and "neoliberal" democracy while others raise alarms about "populist" and "demotic" influence. Still others, as if seeking to shift from the world as we know it to the world as it could be, build sophisticated models for "mini-publics" while fine-tuning procedures and deliberative rules. Outside the university, widespread vertical distrust of politics and politicians is common in advanced democracies, as is a pervasive lack of horizontal trust in each other as resources for long-term constructive social change.[2]

I think that pessimism, abstraction, and distrust are all deeply rooted in the non-participatory and professionally managed public world Americans live in, which we will survey in Chapter 2. Yes, we have social movements, but many civil society groups have become top-down hierarchical organizations that mobilize support, fundraise, and advocate narrowly for an otherwise unlinked membership population.[3] Where once such groups tutored people in the practical communication, interpersonal, and organizational skills useful for effective civic participation, today they are managed by increasingly professionalized staff. Yes we have politics, but in government too, public institutions that could welcome, indeed require, citizen contributions simply do not. Courts, for example, once heard most cases through a jury trial made up of citizens acting—for a few days—as part of their government. Now only 1 to 4 percent of state and federal criminal cases reach the trial stage, with the rest plea bargained or settled.[4] Or consider the decline in the numbers of school boards from 200,000 in the 1930s to 20,000 today, shrinking the access points between community members and a vital democratic institution.[5]

We might suspect, and we wouldn't be wrong, that the organization of modern life is unfriendly to democracy. Our institutions are fields of action, but so often they depress, thwart, and even repel citizen participation. We have good reason to be anxious about concentrations of power and non-transparency in our institutions, good reason to be distrustful and to seek to create wholly different models of democracy. Yet if we know where to look, we will see some powerful examples of democratic innovation that could serve as signposts, at least, for thinking of ways out of our current situation. Collective work in unassuming, everyday places is happening all around us and inviting us in, sometimes even when we don't feel like it.

Rooms

Loathing of airbrushed, sparkle-toothed politicians presiding over public relations events masquerading as town meetings does not translate into fondness for bland, local democratic action. It should.

The photographer Joel Sternfeld traveled the country documenting locations where injustices occurred—murder, vehicular homicide, corporate and political criminality. Here are the camp remains stretched out under the open sky of Cody, Wyoming, where 110,000 Japanese-Americans were imprisoned during World War II; here is the cozy leafy street in Queens where Kitty Genovese was stabbed to death while thirty-eight bystanders failed to come to her aid or call for help; here is the curve in a Los Angeles highway, winding past a neighborhood park toward the Angeles National Forest in the distance, a patch of road where Rodney King was pulled over by police officers in 1991 and savagely beaten. Then, at the very end of *On This Site: Landscape in Memoriam*, after the acknowledgments, almost like an afterword and easy to miss, is a picture of an unassuming place where justice was made; a flawed place for flawed people.

The room is in a mosque on Central Avenue, in the Watts neighborhood of Los Angeles, famous for the six-day riot in 1965. A rust-colored pile carpet covers the floor, two mismatched couches and an overstuffed upholstered chair cluster along one corner in violation of feng shui, an ancient wall heater that looks like a cheese grater runs up one wall, fluorescent lights hum in a stained white spongeboard ceiling—you can almost see divots where bored people have tossed pencils up into it. Three feet below the ceiling, a cord with a dividing cloth wrapped loosely around it is stretched diagonally across the room. The picture, taken at seated eye level from the far end, draws your eye into the warm barren expanse of rust carpet in the center. It is an ugly room, a room you want to get out of as soon as possible. But it was here, Sternfeld notes, that the deadly gang rivalry between the Crips and Bloods came to a halt. The deliberation that gang leaders held, seated in those grungy couches, eying that carpet, listening to the fluorescent lights, saved hundreds of lives in a truce lasting more than a decade.

Rooms like these help us open up a different future. We sit together side by side, we talk, we drink bad coffee, we wait, we listen, we talk some more. It is common to use the words "meeting" and "dialogue," but in rooms like these we make things when we meet and talk. We make safer neighborhoods, we make parents of teenage boys less restless at night, we make emergency rooms and morgues and funeral homes less populated. These dingy rooms are where we find and express our democratic agency, even if we want to linger not on their dusty lumpy furniture gazing out over the rust-colored carpet. "Let's do this," I can hear the participants say, together, before eagerly releasing themselves out of the room into the streets made instantly more peaceful.

People

We are often told that there are some more capable, more knowledgeable, and more skillful at making decisions than others, and this is true up to a point. But nobody has ever found the formula or rulebook for doing the right thing at the right moment in the right way for the right reasons. The one thing that is essential, the ability to *see* others in their differences, similarities, and complexities, is exactly what is denied those who are least proximate to others and sealed off from sharing by their expertise or authority.

The democratic professionals we meet in Chapters 3, 4, and 5 are working in the fields of education, criminal justice, and public administration. Many are situated in institutions such as schools, court complexes, and government agencies in which organizational pressures and professional incentives encourage hierarchical, bureaucratic, non-collaborative decision-making. Yet they push back against these pressures and are motivated to open up their domains—a classroom, police department, city manager's office—to substantive participation by the sometimes nonprofessional and usually non-trained layperson. Real participation means sharing power to define what an institution is producing: education, justice, government. "Power" looks different in different contexts; in a classroom it could be about making a scheduling decision or influencing what is served at lunch; in a prison it could be about taking part in a seminar on Plato; in a local government it could be about being part of a budgeting roundtable. Small or large, I see sharing tasks like these as integral to a more participatory democracy that brings institutional worlds closer to citizens and brings citizens closer to each other, not once every two or four years but routinely every day.

Chapters 3, 4, and 5 are based on a four-year qualitative research project, in which I interviewed more than fifty democratic innovators in these three fields and engaged in participant observation and site visits to better understand how and why they have opened their institutions to participation and how they seek to sustain and grow these practices. Drawing on extensive civic engagement networks connected to organizations devoted to democratic renewal, I found examples of participatory innovation throughout the United States in every region, in small and large cities, and in urban and rural areas. I have tried to embed the qualitative narratives of democratic professionals in a theoretical framework they themselves recognize as valid, drawing from the intellectual resources they indicate as relevant to their work while also seeking connections to a more general understanding of participatory democracy.

It would be a misunderstanding to view these reformers as role models and their institutional contexts as "best practices." Democracy is something people work out together in open-ended, context-sensitive ways without following specific "gold standard" techniques. Playing, non-ironically, on the idea of "best practices" more than a few local governments use "meeting in a box" kits to help community members organize productive neighborhood gatherings.[6] This pragmatic way of reaching disengaged citizens may be necessary, but it also risks trivializing democracy to think you can package it up and mail it out. The chapters to follow are not trying to provide a "democracy in a box." Yet, they also want to appreciate that these sorts of small, sometimes silly techniques can be part of real attempts at sharing power. They alert students of democracy to the need to change the way we operate so as to recognize the value of such ground-level participatory innovations and to engage, constructively, in critique, evaluation, and support. Chapter 6 considers how the motivations that spark reformers and the barriers and openings to innovation they encounter inside institutions might be taken up as issues in democratic inquiry without mythologizing or de-mythologizing leading practitioners. The book's conclusion reflects on the potential of the university in supporting horizontal and grounded forms of inquiry that serve as openings rather than barriers to democratic innovation.

If not "best practices," then what? Maybe the best word is "pathways" or "trails" we can take, or not, shape into new directions, get lost and frustrated on while bitten by mosquitoes, feel close connection to what is most important, sometimes change our lives, or just return home muddy and tired. It is a folksy, organic image to be sure, but notice how many trails exemplify stigmergy, the self-organization of beings acting without a centralized command structure and without specific economic or self-interested motivations.[7] In their making and in their use, trails bring people together in proximity in quasi-voluntary fashion—Thoreau's "one more in the horse track." None are the same but there is an isomorphism across different times and contexts. They can lead to valuable destinations but are also inherently valuable as one can learn about oneself and others and the world around well before any peak or vista or camp is reached. And then again, they may not; you know only by moving along.

What are you going to get out of this book? A little pressure, I hope, to look for participatory innovation where you live, and work, and travel. An invitation to reflect on your own and with others about ways you feel shut out of important problems and how you might begin to work your way in to solutions.

Acknowledgments

IT IS FITTING that this book is a collective effort in practice as well as theory. More people have lent a hand than can be mentioned here, but I want to recognize a few for their help in shaping and sometimes also contesting the ideas presented here.

This book has benefited from discussions in welcoming academic environments at the universities of Canberra, Durham, Edinburgh, Leeds, Oslo, Sheffield, and Tromsø. Thanks are due to a number of colleagues abroad: Henrik Bang, Christopher Bennett, Thom Brooks, the late Nils Christie, John Dryzek, Antony Duff, Selen Ercan, Pamela Fisher, Vidar Halvorsen, and Carolyn Hendriks. Their engagement with this work has improved it immeasurably. Special thanks are due to Ian Loader and Richard Sparks for helping me better understand connections between democracy and criminal justice. Closer to home, I am grateful to Harry Boyte for many conversations about professionals, public work, and participatory democracy.

This research project owes much to supportive but never uncritical co-conspirators at the Kettering Foundation—the "experiment that never stops experimenting." I am indebted to Derek Barker, John Dedrick, Kim Downing, David Holwerk, the late Bob Kingston, Valerie Lemmie, David Mathews, and Stacie Molnar-Main, who have each said something, maybe more than once, that has made its way into this book.

For providing homes for my interviews with democratic innovators, and for terrific editorial guidance, thanks are due to colleagues at the *Boston Review*, *The Good Society*, *The International Journal of Restorative Justice*, and *National Civic Review*. I want to single out Ivo Aertsen and Estelle Zinsstag for their indefatigable support for creative and practical thinking about criminal justice reform.

This book could not have been written without the insights of democratic innovators. I want to especially acknowledge Lauren Abramson, Helen

Beattie, Vanessa Gray, Max Kenner, Kimball Payne, and Donnan Stoicovy. I want to thank them for welcoming me into their work lives, for their time, and for their devotion to the ongoing effort of humanizing and democratizing institutional worlds.

This book is dedicated to Kiran and Neena Dzur, a ray of light and a new hope.

Democracy Inside

Democratic Professionals as Agents of Change

Work as if you live in the early days of a better nation.
—ALASDAIR GRAY

Democratic Professionalism

Democratic professionals are reform-minded innovators working in education, journalism, criminal justice, healthcare, city government, and other fields. They are democratic professionals not because they do democracy professionally, but because they do professionalism democratically. They are democratizing specific parts of our public world that have become professionalized: our schools, newspapers, TV stations, police departments, courts, probation offices, prisons, hospitals, clinics, and government agencies, among others. They use their professional training, capabilities, and authority to help people in their fields of action solve problems together, and even more important, to recognize the kinds of problems they need to solve. They share previously professionalized tasks and encourage lay participation in ways that enhance and enable collective action and deliberation about major social issues inside and outside professional domains.

Professionalism, broadly understood, has important meanings and implications for individuals, groups, and society at large. To be a professional is to have a commitment to competence in a specific field of action— you pursue specialized skills and knowledge so you can act well in difficult situations. Professionals understand their work as having an important normative core: beyond simply earning a living, the work serves society somehow. Sociologists of the professions stress the ways occupations draw boundaries around certain tasks, claim special abilities to handle them, police the ways in which they are discharged, and monitor education and training. Democratic professionalism is an alternative to a conventional form of professionalism

I call *social trustee professionalism*, yet it is also different from some other approaches critical of professional power, which I call the *radical critique*.

The social trustee ideal emerged in the 1860s and held prominence for a century among traditional professions such as law and medicine as well as aspiring professions such as engineering and social work. It holds that professionals have a more general responsibility than just a fiduciary or function-specific obligation to their clients.[1] Of course, professionals are obligated to competently perform their tasks, but they also have general responsibilities that stem from their social status, the trust clients place in them, and the market protection governments have permitted them through licensing and other regulations. As Talcott Parsons put it, "A full-fledged profession must have some institutional means of making sure . . . competence will be put to socially responsible uses."[2] For example, the medical profession heals people, but it also contributes to the larger social goals of curing disease and improving public health. And the legal profession, besides defending their clients' rights, also upholds the social conception of justice.

Social trustee professionals may represent public interests in principle, but in fact this representation is very abstract. Serving "the community" is not seen by professionals as something that requires much say from diverse members of actual, present-day communities. Under the terms of the social trustee model, professionals serve the public through their commitment to high standards of practice, a normative orientation toward a sphere of social concern—doctors and health, lawyers and justice—and self-regulation. The model is held together on the basis of an economy of trust: the public trusts the professionals to self-regulate and determine standards of practice, while the professionals earn that trust by performing competently and adhering to the socially responsible normative orientation. Those public administrators, for example, who see themselves as social trustees assert quite straightforwardly that they are hired to manage issues for which they have specialized training—public budgeting, town planning, and the orchestration of service provision, among others. If their communities disapprove of the way they do their jobs, they can fire them, but true professionals do not need to listen to their communities.

A radical critique emerged in the 1960s, drawing attention to the ways professions can be impediments to the democratic expression of public interests rather than trustworthy representatives. Though aware of the benefits of modern divisions of labor that distribute tasks to different groups of people with specialized training for the sake of efficiency, productivity, and innovation, critics such as Ivan Illich and Michel Foucault worried about task monopolies secured by professionals that block participation, shrink the space of democratic authority, and disable and immobilize citizens who might occupy that space.[3]

Professions shrink the space of democratic authority when they perform public purposes that could conceivably be done by laypeople—as doctors aid human welfare and criminal justice administrators serve needs for social order. Critics stressed that these services and products have public consequences: how they are done affects people not just as individuals but also as members of an ongoing collective. And sometimes professionals quite literally shrink the space of participation by deciding public issues in institutions, far from potential sites of citizen awareness and action. Think of how health-care professionals promote certain kinds of treatment and healing over others and how criminal justice professionals construct complex anger management and life-skills programming for convicted offenders. Professionals can disable and immobilize because, in addition to taking over these tasks, their sophistication in, say, healing or sentencing makes people less comfortable with relying on their own devices for wellness and social order. Professions are professions by virtue of their utilization of abstract, specialized, or otherwise esoteric knowledge to serve social needs such as health or justice. The status and authority of professional work depend on the deference of nonmembers—their acknowledgment that professionals perform these tasks better than untrained others. But with deference comes the risk that members of the general public lose confidence in their own competence—not only where the task itself is concerned, but for making informed collective decisions about issues that relate to professional domains of action.

The social trustee model and radical critique are contrasted with the democratic professionalism alternative in Table 1.1 below.

How can professional actors help mobilize rather than immobilize, expand rather than shrink democratic authority? The radical critique leaves this question largely unexplored. Critics offer few alternatives to social trusteeism for reform-minded practitioners who wish to be both professional and democratic: to de-professionalize or to develop highly self-reflective and acutely power-sensitive forms of professional practice that draw attention to the ways traditional practices and institutions block and manipulate citizens. Yet these reform suggestions fail to register the ways professional power can be constructive for democracy. To the extent that professionals serve as barriers and disablers, they can also, if motivated, serve as barrier removers and enablers. Especially in complex, fast-paced modern societies, professional skills and knowledge help laypeople manage personal and collective affairs. What we

Table 1.1 Ways of Understanding Professionalism

	Social Trustee	Radical Critique	Democratic Professionalism
Main characteristics of a profession	Knowledge, self-regulation, social responsibility	Power to define interests for the public	Commitment to knowledge, but also to co-direction of professional services
Source of professionals' social duties	Group experience, functional purposes, tacit exchange	Interest in retaining status and market security	Professional training and experience, but also from public collaboration
Professionals' view of laypeople	Clients, consumers, wards	Incompetent at high-level tasks	Citizens with a stake in professional decisions
Professionals' ideal role in society	Expert, specialist, guide	De-professionalize, resist temptation to monopolize tasks	Share authority and knowledge through task-sharing
Political role of professions	Protect professional interests and social functions	Disabling intermediary between citizens and institutions	Enabling intermediary between citizens and institutions

need is not an anti-professionalism, but a democratic professionalism oriented toward public capability.[4]

So, how might democratic professionals go about their work? While heeding the conventional obligation to serve social purposes, they also seek to avoid perpetuating the civic disenfranchisement noticed by radical critics of professional power. Democratic professionals relate to society in a particular way: rather than using their skills and expertise as they see fit for the good of others, they aim to understand the world of the patient, the offender, the client, the student, and the citizen on their terms—and then work collaboratively on common problems. They regard the layperson's knowledge and agency as critical components in resolving what can all-too-easily be seen as strictly professional issues: education, government, health, justice, public safety.

Re-thinking Democratic Change

Democratic professionals in the United States are already creating power-sharing arrangements in institutions that are usually hierarchical and non-participatory. Their stories, which will begin in Chapter 3, can help us understand both the obstacles confronted and the resources available for cultural change today. To appreciate these, however, we must release ourselves from the grip of a common view of how and where democratic change happens, notice some underlying social issues as more important and more politically significant than they seem, and avoid some prevailing trends in democratic theory.

Drawing on the historical precedents of the abolition, women's suffrage, labor, civil rights, and student movements, discussion of democratic change typically focuses on the power of people joined together in common cause and pressing for major legislative action. Core factors in the process include leadership; mobilization; organizational capacity; consciousness-raising; forms of protest such as strikes, marches, and sit-ins; and electoral pressure on political parties and candidates.

While our default perspective is crucial for understanding some vital types of democratic action—as, for example, the Black Lives Matter movement has recently demonstrated—it is state-centric and privileges resources and commitments that are exogenous to daily life. Political action appears as a burst of collective energy that then dissipates after certain legal or policy targets are met: slavery abolished, voting rights for women established, the eight-hour day guaranteed, military conscription for Vietnam ended. A large enough number of people temporarily leave their everyday routines to join in a collective effort. For this reason, Sheldon Wolin has called democratic movements "fugitive," since at the end of the protest, or strike, or campaign, most people return to their families, neighborhoods, and workplaces, leaving the business of government to insiders.[5]

Yet some purposeful democratic action is not fugitive. Harry Boyte, John McKnight, and other students of community organizing have drawn attention to the public work of self-directing community groups that band together to secure affordable housing, welcome new immigrant groups, and repair common areas such as parks and playgrounds.[6] Though deeply relevant to many neighborhoods' quality of life, such public work barely registers in the mass media and academia because it does not usually expend its energy on law and policy.

Even less noticed are the alterations democratic professionals are making to their organizations: they take their public responsibilities seriously and listen carefully to those outside their walls and those at all levels of their internal hierarchy in order to foster physical proximity between formerly separated individuals, encourage co-ownership of problems previously seen as beyond laypeople's ability or realm of responsibility, and seek out opportunities for collaborative work between laypeople and professionals. We fail to see these activities as politically significant because they do not fit our conventional picture of democratic change. As if to repay the compliment, the democratic professionals I have interviewed in the fields of criminal justice, public administration, and K-12 education rarely use the concepts employed by social scientists and political theorists. Lacking an overarching ideology, they make it up as they go along, developing roles, attitudes, habits, and practices that open calcified structures up to greater participation. Their democratic action is thus endogenous to their occupational routine, often involving those who would not consider themselves activists or even engaged citizens. As Table 1.2 indicates, democratic professionalism offers a different path to democratic change than social movements.

Though they belong to practitioner networks and engage in ongoing streams of print, online, and face-to-face dialogue, the democratic professionals I have met do not form a typical social movement. Rather than mobilizing fellow activists and putting pressure on government officeholders to make new laws or rules, or convening temporary participatory processes such as citizens' juries or deliberative polls, democratic professionals make direct changes to their institutional domains piece by piece, practice by practice. In the trenches all around us they are renovating and reconstructing schools, clinics, prisons, and other seemingly inert bodies.

In Chapter 3 we will meet Donnan Stoicovy, a principal in State College, Pennsylvania, who turned her kindergarten through 5th grade institution into an explicitly "democratic" school by designing curricula and internal

Table 1.2 Two Paths of Democratic Change

	Social Movements	Democratic Professionals
Driven by:	Cognitive shifts	Proximity
Sites:	Outside formal bodies	Inside formal bodies
Goals:	Law or policy change	Role, habit, practice change
Participation:	Optional	Not fully voluntary

structures to encourage student voice and participation in setting school policies. In Chapter 4 we will hear from Lauren Abramson, who convenes community justice conferences in some of the most distressed neighborhoods in Baltimore, Maryland, to address harmful actions before they become formal crimes and enter into the criminal justice system. In Chapter 5 we will learn from democratic public administrator Kimball Payne how racial tensions fueling distrust were mitigated through widespread citizen action in Lynchburg, Virginia. Stoicovy, Abramson, Payne, and the other democratic professionals we will meet are changing routine, everyday practices where we all live and work. Their democratic practices are not, therefore, "fugitive" in Wolin's terms because they are part of our daily life.

Democratic professionals have leverage on the social world, but it differs from that of the political actors and movement organizers we are used to. The energy involved is not a large burst but a slow burn fueled not by a shift in public consciousness, but through load-bearing work that fosters relations of proximity within classrooms, conference rooms, and administrative offices, spaces newly reopened to the public as civic spaces.[7] This proximity in public space—getting close enough to see and understand others as fellow citizens— is taken for granted, and yet it is in astonishingly short supply. We live in a democracy, but it is very easy to go through life without ever working democratically on a public problem with others different from oneself in race, class, or education.

Asocial Structures and the Proximity Deficit

Even in the first half of the nineteenth century, astute observers noticed that coexisting alongside highly participatory elements of American democracy, such as frequent elections, town meetings, and jury trials, were significant evasions of civic responsibility and a cultivated lack of political awareness. Alexis de Tocqueville saw what he called "individualism" as a common vice of the new world: not the selfishness or egoism he was accustomed to in Europe, but a cool conscious retreat from the public sphere into the familial private domain. Americans could go off into the forests of Michigan, build cabins, farm, hunt, and live quietly without contributing much to the outside world or relying on it.[8] Tocqueville saw this as a personal, if ultimately mistaken, choice made possible by relative equality of conditions and bountiful natural resources.

John Dewey, writing a hundred years later in his 1927 book, *The Public and Its Problems*, worried similarly about the difficulties individuals had in joining up in collective action. For Dewey, though, it was the complexity of the public world and not the inducements of the private life that constituted the main problem. The modern public, he wrote, was in eclipse, too "scattered, mobile, and manifold" to find itself. To be sure, twentieth-century Americans inherited a participatory infrastructure—town meetings, local control, competitive elections—but it was inadequate for an era of urban populations, large-scale corporations, and cross-regional issues. Democracy, Dewey thought, "consists in having a responsible share according to capacity in forming and directing the activities of the groups to which one belongs and in participating according to need in the values which the groups sustain."[9] But how could individuals awaken to this responsibility and adequately discharge it under conditions that bewilder them and obscure common interests?

Now, ninety years later, the public is even more scattered, mobile, and manifold. Public squares, parks, and other places of unexpected meetings and common experiences are often displaced by commercialized private spaces.[10] Sociologists write of contemporary social structures that, paradoxically, de-structure common life, distance us from one another, and make it increasingly hard for us to interact in anything but a partial, superficial, and self-selecting fashion. Zygmunt Bauman coins a term, *adiaphorization*, for how modern society exerts a "soporific influence" that prevents "individuals from awakening to their 'mutual dependencies' and so to their mutual responsibilities."[11] This helps update Tocqueville's and Dewey's analyses: individualism under modern conditions of adiaphorization is not merely a matter of choosing to retreat from the complicated, unattractive public world to a more attractive private life; it is, rather, a social aspect of a public world that has itself become narrowly segmented:

> [I]t is not that the solidary life is in trouble because of the inborn self-interest of "inadequately socialized" individuals. The opposite is the case: individuals tend to be self-centered and self-engrossed (and so morally blind and ethically uninvolved or incompetent) because of the slow yet relentless waning of the collectivities to be solidary with. It is because there is little reason to be solidary, "the others" turn into strangers—and of the strangers, as every mother keeps telling her child, one should beware; and best of all keep one's distance and not talk to them at all.[12]

Modern ways of life structure our perceptions of one another and disable us in various ways from handling common problems.

The Man in the Park

A good example of this social production of distance comes from Nils Christie, who asks us to imagine two apartment buildings overlooking a park.[13] The "house of turbulence" was never fully finished because the builder went bankrupt. The occupants, who had already bought their flats, were forced to finish them on their own and to complete the common areas too: the sidewalks, grounds, and entryway. They became organized, created committees and teams to divide up the labor, and in the process came to know each other. In the "house of perfection," by contrast, finished on time and up to standards, neighbors do not know each other, have no history of common work, and therefore no shared language of problem-solving.

Now think of how the tenants of these different buildings perceive a troubling event. A slightly disheveled man walks into the park carrying a sack of beer and mumbling to nobody in particular. He drinks and sits in the sun. Schoolchildren done for the day eventually wander over and play nearby. After a while the man gets up to relieve himself, all within view of the children. Residents of the house of perfection see what appears to be a social problem: public drunkenness and sexual exposure. They immediately turn to the social problem-solvers, in this case the police. The act is interpreted as a "crime," which creates further distance between the man in the park and the residents of the house of perfection. By contrast, the residents of the house of turbulence see Brian, son of Anna and the victim of a childhood accident that has left him a little strange but harmless. When they see him drinking in the park and urinating with children around they do not see a specific social problem, a crime: they see a complex person with a particular history. They try to find Anna to help, not a police officer.

Clearly these are metaphors not ethnographic descriptions, but Christie is pointing to how modern ways of life structure our perceptions of each other and disable us in various ways from handling common problems. "If I am acquainted with my neighbours and have some sort of network close to me," Christie writes, "I have an easy time if some youngsters misbehave in my hallway. I can call for someone who might know some of them, or I can turn to the athletic neighbour one floor up—or perhaps better—I can ask for help from the little lady I know as particularly good at handling local conflicts." "But without a network," he continues, "and with all the information on the increase of crime in mind, I would have locked the door

and called the police. I would thereby have created conditions both for encouraging unwanted behaviour, and for giving that unwanted behaviour the
meaning of crime."[14]

It was accidental rather than planned, but the house of turbulence is an
example of what I call "rational disorganization." Bringing people together
in close proximity, these very ordinary structures foster communication, encourage task-sharing, and allow a different perspective of those on the margins
precisely because it is more porous to those on the margins.

Neoliberal Elites and Mini-publics but No Citizens

In the face of daunting asocial structures, the decline of broad-based organizations noted earlier, and other barriers to collective action including,
as we will see, concentrations of economic power, influential scholars
have been caught up in two strong intellectual currents: pessimism and
proceduralism. These viewpoints are not wrong—indeed there is much of
real value to draw from both—but each is incomplete and self-defeating
in its own way. From these perspectives it is difficult to articulate a viable
democratic agency and to name people and practices that could establish
links between institutions and citizens, and between citizens and citizens.
They ignore the work of democratic professionals entirely, as it occupies no
place of any significance.

Pessimism

Sheldon Wolin, for example, describes formal democratic institutions that are
manipulated by insiders held sway by powerful economic interests: an oligarchy in democratic clothing. Like other modern states, he argues, the United
States has constitutionalized democracy, placing the demos on the sidelines of
real authority. Party politics agitates and mobilizes during elections, but then
fades without much improvement to people's lives. Voters are left disgruntled
and ultimately resigned to apathy.

The facile translation of economic power into the business of government is a part of a deeper problem at the heart of modern state structure.
For Wolin, the institutionalization of politics that emerged early on as
societies grew more complex signals the death of "the political," the end of
democracy.

Institutionalization brings not only settled practices regarding such matters as authority, jurisdiction, accountability, procedures, and processes but routinization, professionalization. . . . Institutionalization depends on the ritualization of the behavior of both rulers and ruled to enable the formal functions of the state—coercion, revenue collection, policy, mobilization of the population for war, law making, punishment, and enforcement of the laws—to be conducted on a continuing basis. It tends to produce internal hierarchies, to restrict experience, to associate political experience with institutional experience, and to inject an esoteric element into politics.[15]

Because of such constraints, democracy becomes a fugitive as formal state institutions develop, only to surface from time to time in "transgressive" moments when those excluded attempt to reconstitute the institutional rules. Democracy is a "moment rather than a form" for Wolin and perpetually on the run.[16] Historically, as soon as the demos achieves success in translating numbers into real political power, norms and rules emerge inside institutions that begin to sap its strength. Those with economic power shield their advantages by fixing institutional boundaries to block incursions by those who only have numbers on their side. In such a system routine political activity has low value and high costs for the leisureless who make up the demos, so they are left on the sidelines to agitate and to sporadically rise up when conditions are apt.[17]

Democracy in America, for Wolin, has always been anti- and extra-institutional. From the resistance and then revolutionary movement in the eighteenth century, to the Jacksonian, abolition, suffragette, union, and populist currents of the nineteenth century, to the civil rights and the youth movements of the twentieth century, American democratic politics has been an "irruptive," "episodic" force.[18] Wolin believes in the continuing restorative power of democratic action, but sees its viability only outside regular interventions in state institutions and formal politics. Environmental, fair-trade, and antiglobalization activism fosters commonality of purpose and presses for reforms that directly contribute to the well-being of ordinary citizens. Community efforts at the local level are another example, where citizens team up to monitor dangerous neighborhoods, oversee school performance, and tend to common spaces: "small politics, small projects, small business, much improvisation, and hence anathema to centralization."[19] In Wolin's view, democratic participation within the established forms, rules, and procedures of settled institutions becomes apolitical, attenuated in its connection with the authentic politics out of doors. "Democracy needs to be reconceived," he writes, "as something other than a form of government: as a mode of being which is conditioned by bitter experience, doomed to succeed only temporarily, but is a recurrent possibility as long as the memory of the political survives."[20]

Wendy Brown follows Wolin in drawing attention to the ways the ideas embedded in contemporary institutions such as efficiency, entrepreneurialism, and self-care actively discourage collective power-sharing. This "neoliberal" rationality, she believes, has weakened the political culture and has produced what she calls "the undemocratic citizen." "This is the citizen," she writes, "who loves and wants neither freedom nor equality, even of a liberal sort; the citizen who expects neither truth nor accountability in governance and state actions; the citizen who is not distressed by exorbitant concentrations of political and economic power, routine abrogations of the rule of law, or distinctly undemocratic formulations of national purpose at home and abroad."[21]

Brown points to how social, political, and economic relations have all become saturated by market thinking: "The political sphere, along with every other dimension of contemporary existence, is submitted to an economic rationality . . . not only is the human being configured exhaustively as homo oeconomicus, all dimensions of human life are cast in terms of a market rationality."[22] This means that "every action and policy" is assessed in terms of profit and loss: increasingly sophisticated and invasive economic metrics of efficiency and utility are used everywhere. Even more pervasively, neoliberalism "develops institutional practices and rewards for enacting this vision."[23] These include for profit charter schools, outsourced social welfare programs, and independent for-profit military contractors, among many other examples.

The model citizen under these conditions, argues Brown, is the one who makes "good choices," the "individual entrepreneurs and consumers whose moral autonomy is measured by their capacity for 'self care'—their ability to provide for their own needs and service their own ambitions."[24] Brown writes of the "troubling possibility of an abject, unemancipatory, and anti-egalitarian subjective orientation amongst a significant swathe of the American populace."[25] This is not just a "feeling," a sense of "apathy," or "detachment" but reflects a very real loss of collective sovereignty. An example of this loss is what Brown calls the "depoliticization of social problems"; neoliberal citizens have grown up in a social world where public problems are not public at all: "the project of navigating the social becomes entirely one of discerning, affording, and procuring a personal solution to every socially produced problem. . . . If we have a problem, we look to a product to solve it; indeed, a good deal of our lives is devoted to researching, sharing, procuring, and upgrading these solutions."[26] Another example is what she calls the "governed citizen," the "extensive governance and heavy administrative authority" in evidence today— from intensive monitoring for security purposes, in school, marketplaces, and on the street, to invasive measuring and testing in public and private workplaces.[27]

This kind of "depoliticization" has such strong economic, political, and social forces behind it that Brown holds it to be the dominant cultural mode in today's democracy. Indeed, Brown's analysis is more deeply pessimistic than Wolin's, as she argues neoliberalism's counter-democratic impact is felt in the public sphere outside the state as much as within formal government institutions. Contemporary democracy, in her view, is fugitive inside and out. While pointing out significant flaws and failings in institutions and among citizens themselves, most importantly by identifying systemic counter-democratic pressures, these theories offer little by way of scaffolding for citizens interested in democratic agency and renewal.

Proceduralism

While pessimists draw attention to the counter-democratic tendencies of the public sphere, another major school of contemporary political thought bypasses actually existing political practice and seeks to create altogether new terrain. Moreover, they appear to be building precisely the scaffolding missing from pessimists' work. Archon Fung captures this tendency well by his term "mini-public:" "self-consciously organized public deliberations" and "highly artifactual efforts" that create "instances of more perfect public spheres, often out of whole cloth."[28] These are, in his view, "among the most promising actual constructive efforts for civic engagement and public deliberation in contemporary politics."[29]

One example of a mini-public is the deliberative democratic poll designed by James Fishkin. These bring a few hundred carefully selected people together for a number of hours to discuss a particular issue, such as public utility rates, public education, or criminal justice. Sophisticated random selection procedures are followed to make sure the population inside this mini-public does not differ in meaningful ways from the public at large outside. Over the course of the event participants engage in structured small-group discussions and choice-making exercises to help them sort through their positions on an issue. Experts and officials are present in large group sessions to answer questions. Attendees are surveyed at the beginning and the end of the event to note changes in opinion. The general idea, Fishkin says, is to put "the whole country (or the whole region or the whole state or the whole town) in one room where it can think."[30]

Another sort of mini-public are advisory forums such as "citizens' juries" charged with offering advice on policy priorities. These assemble small groups also selected carefully so they represent the public at large. Participants are often chosen on the basis of characteristics such as age, gender, ethnicity, employment, education, and income levels, while avoiding people affiliated with special interest groups, government agencies, and political parties. They then meet with expert witnesses and engage in question-and-answer sessions with relevant government officials. After listening to experts and questioning officials, the jurors deliberate and come to some group agreement on what advice to present.

Mini-publics have a number of advantages and appear, at least on the surface, to open up possibilities for change unappreciated by more pessimistic theorists. Though not without expenses—for randomization procedures, facilitators' and participants' time, transportation, and venue—they are certainly cheaper and less time-intensive than large-scale action. They are highly mobile and versatile: deliberative polls and citizens' juries have been used all across the United States on many different topics, hosted by government agencies, news-media outlets, universities, and nongovernmental organizations (NGOs). When they go well, they can help clarify citizens' preferences on important topics, increase knowledge of the specific topics discussed, improve general civic awareness and interest, and build trust across social differences. If mini-public activities are covered by the news media, they can also spread awareness even further into the broader public sphere.

At the same time, however, mini-publics are severely limited as democratic bodies and may serve more as symbols than substantive links between citizens and institutions and between citizens and citizens. Participants are not sharing power over collective decisions because such decisions are not typically part of their charter. While their activities are educative and conducive to trust-building, no small virtues, they are nonetheless usually "just talk." Participants are not making decisions with any impact on people's lives, and what they say inside the mini-public has little influence on the general public and on politicians and officials inside formal institutions.[31] Though a few examples of linked or empowered forums in other countries, such as the British Columbia Citizens' Assembly, are widely discussed and appreciated by practitioners, deliberative forums in the United States are typically freestanding experiments with little capacity to present advice to official bodies holding decision-making power, not to mention exercise any actual decision-making power of their own. Indeed, it is somewhat of a misnomer to call these forums "mini-publics" because they are not really public spheres: academic researchers, NGOs, and government agencies bring them into being—recall Fung's comment about their "highly artifactual" nature. Mini-publics owe their existence to the discretion of these entities; they are therefore ephemeral, top-down creations rather than emerging from lasting commitments forged at the grass-roots level or from historical political settlements.[32]

One could say that the time is not yet ripe and that eventually, given enough critical mass and with the right kinds of systemic linkages, as John Dryzek writes, "mini-publics would not be isolated exercises" but instead "would have multifaceted and multidirectional relationships with other actors in the larger public sphere as well as government."[33] This may be so, but for it to be so both a greater respect for citizen agency from within the world of institutions and a greater pressure to engage in action on the part of citizens must be developed. Crucial dimensions of the public sphere and the world of government must turn from repelling meaningful citizen agency to attracting it.

Contrast the mini-public to a much older entity that once held a leading role in the American participatory infrastructure: the trial jury. This is "public" because it is a space guaranteed to lay citizens: officials cannot take it away. On the jury, citizens talk, to be sure, but through this talk they also bear responsibility for real decisions that have an impact on others' lives. Citizens produce something: a verdict. This verdict exists in time and space in a way that the survey-responses of the mini-publics do not. There is a political history and public record being created by juries but not by mini-publics; indeed, though they decide only the specific case in front of them, the cumulative decisions of juries can be said to make policy.[34]

Though they appear to offer more possibilities for change than pessimistic commentators on American democracy, proceduralists deliver less than promised. While pessimists describe very real hurdles to democratic action today, proceduralists bypass the real world and offer little to address deep gaps between citizens and institutions and between citizens and each other. Discursive acuity in a mini-public is a temporary palliative to the chronic absence of publicness that has hollowed out all our major institutions. Indeed, neither school of thought adequately describes democratic agency from a horizontal grounding in civic experience. Both, in their own ways, see ordinary citizen agency as deeply flawed and in need of repair by experts in systems and process. Neither theory embraces the collaborative aspect of democratic professional work making institutions less asocial in this difficult, but far from hopeless, time. Nor do they properly value the civic agency illustrated by Christie's house of turbulence or the ugly Los Angeles room—these stories of people working through conflicts, meeting their neighbors' needs, making more peaceful streets, at least for a few months or years. Pessimists and proceduralists do not provide enough of the conceptual tools needed to get a purchase on asocial structures that surround us or to identify sources of constructive power and long-term sustainable innovation.

Starting Where We Are, Using What We Have

What democratic professionals contribute is better registered by democratic theorists swimming away from the intellectual currents of pessimism and proceduralism. Though aware of contemporary democratic deficits and conscious of how imperfect ground-level political action can be in the absence of structuring norms, these theorists chart categories of democratic action that hold promise for wider, institutional impact. Where proceduralists focus on alternative spheres of discussion and pessimists hope against hope for collective action outside formal institutions, theorists such as Pierre Rosanvallon and Henrik Bang are interested in revitalizing democratic structures and nurturing citizen agency that can connect with existing institutions.

Addressing power disparities between insiders occupying formal institutions and outsiders looking in, these grounded democratic thinkers also take up the problem of social separation and disengagment. Like many scholars, they do not assume an active and alert public ready to press on government to represent its interests. As we have noted and as pessimistic theorists rightly point out, in many respects, citizens in advanced democracies live in less participatory, more professionally managed, and more socially fragmented public worlds than previous generations. And like proceduralists insist, specific forms and practices are needed to address these circumstances and bring people into deliberative spaces. But grounded theorists start in the earthly reality of the here and now, with specific paths and trails built by citizens, activists, and other reformers. Grounded theorists are less concerned with norms of deliberative dialogue and more interested in the non-cognitive structures and practices that are bringing detached individuals closer together right now; for them, proximity takes some priority to rules of rational discourse, and the action takes place in and around existing institutions not in the parallel world of "artifactual" mini-publics.

Citizens and Counter Powers

Rosanvallon describes what he calls "counter powers" possessed by regular citizens that supplement, correct, and sometimes interfere with the normal workings of representative democratic government. They operate on the margins of formal institutions and are not part of the normal electoral process or organized politics. Nevertheless, non-elite citizens take up considerable roles as watchdogs, veto-wielders, and judges.

Popular oversight, the watchdog role, comes in three forms: vigilance, denunciation, and evaluation. Vigilance simply means being "watchful, alert, and on guard" and involves "monitoring"—permanent close scrutiny of the actions of government."[35] Traditionally done by journalists, editors, academics, and others similarly situated, vigilance is also often carried out by large and small activist groups. Denunciation means bringing into view some violation of public trust or abuse of authority. As with vigilance, members of the press, mass media, social media, and online networks are particularly active here; investigative journalism drawing attention to specific flawed decisions by a named group of actors is a classic case of denunciation. Evaluation, the third form of popular oversight, "involves carefully researched, technically sophisticated, often quantified judgment of specific actions or more general policies. The goal is to bring expertise to bear on governmental management in order to improve its quality and efficiency."[36] Citizens "bring their own practical expertise to bear, making use of information not available to decision-makers remote from the place where the consequences of their decisions are actually felt."[37] Activists working in small associations or as part of larger networks online and off exercise all these forms of oversight. A more institutionalized example of evaluation is the Citizen Initiative Review process established by the Oregon Legislature, in which a representative group of citizens meets to discuss initiatives that will appear on the ballots in the next election. They study the language of the proposed laws, meet with supporters and opponents, hear from nonpartisan experts in the field, and deliberate together to produce a one-page analysis—including main findings and arguments for and against—that will be disseminated to all voters.[38]

Laypeople exercise prevention, the veto power, when they engage in various forms of "passive resistance, tactical withdrawal, or clever circumvention of rules" available to regular citizens, not to mention more direct confrontations with authority such as "rebellions, riots, and other spontaneous uprisings."[39] Black Lives Matter street protests across the country, often sparked by police actions, are examples of direct actions, and many other widespread instances of rule and policy avoidance occur every day via unscrutinized citizen circumventions.

Judgment is best exemplified by the role of the juror, which as we have noted is decreasingly available in today's courtroom, but, as Rosanvallon points out, also "extends beyond the strict framework of the law and the courts. It includes detailed and reasoned evaluation, a process of examination leading to the resolution of a question."[40] "[C]itizens act as judges when they participate in various kinds of investigation, whether through the media or as political activists."[41] Courtwatch groups in the United States and other countries, for example, make judgments about trials and proceedings. Citizens attend trials and other court proceedings in particular districts with respect to certain kinds of cases, such as domestic violence or racial bias. Courtwatchers follow the progress of the legal arguments, look at how well judges and attorneys comport themselves, take notes, and report to a broader audience outside important details about what has taken place inside the courtroom. Many programs gather local data and publicize comparisons to state and national norms. As we will discuss later, judgment is also provided by community-based informal justice programs, such as those developed in schools to handle issues such as bullying without reliance on the formal criminal justice system.

Everyday Makers

Henrik Bang, drawing on a long-term qualitative study of political activism in an inner city neighborhood in Copenhagen, joins Rosanvallon in rejecting the view of contemporary citizens as flawed, apathetic, and lacking agency. Instead, he sees them as alienated from traditional forms of politics in which they have no serious roles to play. Agreeing with pessimistic theorists that policymaking institutions and elections tend to shut citizens out, Bang also points to governance scholarship indicating how incapacities in the formal system incline officials and agencies to seek citizen input. "We witness a change in governance and participation," he writes, "from an emphasis on a mode of deliberation and decisionmaking to a mode of action, sparked by the increased complexity of society and accompanying escalating reflexivity of individuals wanting to make a more direct impact on policy articulation and delivery than the formal representative structures of collective decision-making can offer."[42] In this new "network mode of political governance," Bang argues, "effective, goal-orientated action seems to matter more than the process of deliberation."[43]

Unlike the "fugitive" and "de-democratized" citizens pessimists describe, Bang points to new "cause-oriented critical citizens and forms of micro-personal political activity" that "are far less organized, institutionalized and collectivized than are those of the civic traditions of representative democracy." Far from lacking agency, these new citizens "favour a more spontaneous, ad hoc and individualized mode of activism which they have chosen, exactly because the old ones allow them only to be passive or active."[44] Wary of both overweening community ties and state demands, Bang notes that the citizens he has met "are much more interested in enhancing their personal and common capacities for self-governance and co-governance, right where they are, than in submitting themselves to an abstract social norm or mode of state citizenship. They prefer a 'thin' form of democratic political community that allows for the reciprocal acceptance and recognition of difference. They also consider 'strong,' effective and responsive government from above a permanent threat to their self-governance and co-governance."[45]

Bang names two newly relevant types of democratic agent, the "expert citizen" and the "everyday maker." Expert citizens are grass-roots activists who take on political projects as central to their work and life. They gain practical expertise in particular policy areas, and develop skills in negotiating with officials and bureaucrats and in organizing interested but less devoted fellow citizens. They do not have an oppositional consciousness, says Bang. "What is of concern to them is no longer fighting the system . . . but rather gaining access to the bargaining processes which go on between public authorities and various experts from private and voluntary organizations."[46] To be effective, the expert citizen "knows that one must be as professional as the others."[47] From the perspective of those inside government, expert citizens can be extremely useful, "providing a fund of knowledge about how to deal systematically with complex everyday problems."[48]

Everyday makers, like expert citizens, "are project-oriented and want to deal with common concerns concretely and personally rather than abstractly and ideologically."[49] They eschew party politics and formal political institutions, but they are not apathetic. "Typically, they think globally but want to act locally, because they want to do things by themselves, where they are, on their own terms and for their own purposes."[50] Yet they also do not wish to devote their lives to political action; unlike expert citizens they tend to steer clear of elite networking. "They believe that lay involvement is valuable in itself as a way to develop oneself as a reflective being with a sense of commonality."[51] The credo of everyday makers, writes Bang, is the following:

do it yourself;
do it where you are;
do it for fun, but also because you find it necessary;
do it ad hoc or part time;
do it concretely, instead of ideologically;
do it self-confidently and show trust in yourself;
do it with the system, if need be.[52]

The everyday maker does not see herself as a victim of neoliberalism and would not tolerate merely being polled about her deliberative preferences. This "is a strong, self-relying and capable individual," Bang insists, "who conceives of politics and policy as the concrete and direct handling of diversity, difference and dispute concerning live political problems."[53] Such people have extremely practical and non-ideological kinds of agency, viewing "the institutions and networks that they meet on their way more as features of their everyday life than as properties of government." "They do not regard these institutions and networks as either external or coercive state institutions that continuously have to be resisted," notes Bang. Neither are they part of any social movement or robust collective effort, as they do not "look upon themselves as moral beings with a strong sense of social solidarity. They rather conceive of themselves as political individuals living with, and in, such institutions and networks of political decision and action, conditioning both their self-governance and their empowerment."[54]

Like the citizens and groups exercising their counter powers, everyday makers are in evidence all around us, if we have the framework to see them. They are working as part-time volunteers in libraries, organizing projects in schools, sitting on review boards in hospitals and clinics, staffing temporary offices for the production of newsletters, and planning and monitoring parades and other local events. Because we are normally looking for formal politics or social movement activism we do not tend to see everyday makers as democratic agents, but they are. They may not be proposing laws or challenging policies, but they are making public institutions more transparent and more responsive to human needs.

The Civic Leverage of Professionals

Bang and Rosanvallon's fine-grained ground-level discussions of democratic agency are useful for understanding what professionals might contribute to the world as we know it. I want to underscore, however, two points that linger too far in the background of their arguments. The first has to do with the voluntary nature of the citizen activity they discuss. Everyday makers are not actually making things every day; indeed, they freely choose what projects to devote their energies to, where they will be active and when, and just how much time and effort to expend. The same is true for Rosanvallon's citizens taking up counter powers, which are exercised, whenever they are, at the discretion of those deciding to be vigilant, or denunciatory, or evaluatory. Therefore, what might need to be "made" or "denounced" or "evaluated" may go unaddressed for lack of interested and alert agents. Second, how interested and alert such citizens are with regard to others not like them is an open question. Because what they do is freely chosen, they may never have to face people or topics that challenge their perspectives or routines. Everyday makers and counter-power exercising citizens may never have their complacencies and conventionalities challenged by otherness.

These issues indicate why the leverage democratic professionals can exert is particularly important. When they open up environments that have become sealed off to meaningful civic activity, when they share power over tasks and responsibility for problems they cannot fully handle on their own, they can bring citizens together in a *partially* voluntary way. Of course, they do not want to build "houses of turbulence" to do so, but they do wish to create pressures and routines that encourage face-to-face contact and communication across social differences, to rationally disorganize institutions that will foster routine everyday democratic agency. In so doing, they develop a more widespread culture of responsibility for others. Their efforts are easily missed, however, by those looking elsewhere for democratic change and by those skeptical about whether institutions can become participatory in any meaningful fashion.

Proximity and Responsibility

Democratic professionals who bring laypeople together to produce justice, education, public health and safety, and government—when done routinely in the normal social environment—are helping backfill the erosion of contemporary public life. Some contribute by repairing our frayed participatory infrastructure: the traditional town meetings, public hearings, jury trials, and citizen oversight committees. Others are remodeling these old forms and creating new civic spaces; democratic professionals who share load-bearing work in schools, public health clinics, city governments, and even prisons are innovators who are expanding, not just conserving, American democracy.

Managers, officials, and mid-level professionals all too easily seal themselves off from clients, taxpayers, and patients; they serve and treat people without fully understanding them. They privilege speed, efficiency, and cost containment and employ hierarchies and divisions of labor. These internal arrangements create distance between organizations and citizens, neglecting the democratic value of proximity. To restore it, institutions must edge closer to the public work already being done by lay citizens and community groups, whether they are exercising counter powers or acting as everyday makers. To borrow concepts from Max Weber, proximity requires adjusting formal institutional rationality to accommodate, appreciate, and act upon the substantive rationality of citizens already making a difference in the world.[55]

David Mathews aptly calls this process *alignment* and has shown how institutions and citizens alike gain from collaborative rather than technocratic working relations.[56] Alignment, Mathews points out, demands more than being "accountable," or "transparent," or "professional" to citizens on terms defined by professionals, but it "doesn't require massive reform or asking overworked professionals to take on an extra load of new duties."[57] Rather, it means an organization must rethink a social trustee orientation and recognize the value of citizens' attempts to solve problems on their own. Given the right kind of institutional culture, alignment can result in some organizational activities actually being steered by values and objectives brought in by laypeople. Stoicovy's democratic school in State College, which we will discuss in Chapter 3, aligns to the issues and concerns brought in by active students empowered to use their voice. Abramson's community justice conferences in Baltimore noted in Chapter 4 align the criminal justice process to the contours of particular neighborhood conflicts. Payne's study circles revealed practical ideas for dealing with long-standing issues of racial injustice in Lynchburg's local government, as we will see in Chapter 5. In each of these cases, too, alignment of an institutional world to social and personal worlds gives meaning to everyday making while also challenging people to see one another as fellow citizens.

Proximity also involves bringing citizens together who had not planned to be together, had not joined a group or party or network. Kids in Stoicovy's school are students, not party members; participants in Abramson's conferences are neighbors, not association members; attendees at Payne's racial justice study circles are citizens, not advocates. Sometimes the substantive rationality that serves as a valuable corrective to technocratic or instrumental rationality doesn't arise from citizens' fully formed intentions and interests. Instead, it develops within institutions, through practices that encourage lay involvement and power-sharing. This sort of action is particularly important for treating issues people would rather ignore because they think they have no direct interest at stake or because they conceive of them as shameful or distasteful in some way—such as incarceration rates or prison conditions, for example. Proximity encourages co-ownership of processes, problems, and solutions that usually fall to the experts to handle. And it's precisely the fact that citizens neither demand nor desire co-ownership (at least in some cases) that makes proximity so important as a force for democratic change. Co-ownership is a bulwark against apathy and learned civic irresponsibility.

This latter kind of proximity, which brings previously un-networked citizens together face to face, is less commonly discussed as relevant to democratization than the former type, which seeks to close the distance between citizens and institutions. So, it may help to say more about how, exactly, this interpersonal proximity works and why its effects would be discernibly democratic. Consider the capital jury, the body that must decide whether a death sentence is appropriate. Even though they only seat death-qualified jurors who believe the penalty is just in principle, such juries choose death significantly less often than the public-opinion statistics on Americans' views of the death penalty would predict.[58] It is not discourse about the validity of the death penalty or consciousness-raising that causes this discrepancy, but rather shared responsibility for a grave decision and proximity to the living, breathing person being sentenced. Likewise, standard Gallup-style public-opinion polls about punishment in the United States register generally severe attitudes, but when qualitative researchers provide context-rich narrative descriptions of particular offenders, respondents' sentencing opinions become more moderate.[59]

Consider another criminal justice example of the power of proximity. In the aftermath of the Oklahoma City bombings, Bud Welch, whose twenty-three-year-old daughter Julie Marie died in the Murrah Federal Building, wanted nothing more than the death of Timothy McVeigh. While grieving he decided, almost reflexively—perhaps to get answers, to share something about his suffering, or some other less conscious motive—to visit McVeigh's father. While at the house he saw a picture of the son as a youth and remarked, without thinking, "God, what a good looking kid." In an instant, as McVeigh's father began to weep at the comment, the two men achieved a kind of shared humanity. Welch left knowing that he could not support the death penalty for McVeigh. "Nothing would be gained by adding number 168 to the 167 already dead," he told an interviewer.

We have an underutilized capacity to connect, to see humanity even in the darkest corners of public life, to find common cause across our many legitimate differences and allegiances. It may be utopian to think that sharing public responsibility in public spaces will lead to robustly communitarian civic relationships—many of us, after all, may not want to belong to such a thick society—but perhaps it is enough if these task-sharing opportunities serve as an antidote to the bureaucracy, compartmentalization of responsibility, and division of labor that make it difficult to recognize other people not like us as our fellow citizens.[60] As we see in the capital jury example, these juries are a way that courts share responsibility for justice; they circulate laypeople into a professionalized institution, and through the unanimity rule, make sure everyone's voice matters in a structured, sober, and reflective way. Fellow citizens sit in judgment regarding other citizens at their worst moments.

Likewise, we need to see our institutions as fields of social action, as our co-productions rather than as fixed forms. To do this, however, we must get them to stop thinking and acting for us. This is a job for democratic professionals, so therefore it is a job for those of us entering professions to think critically and energetically about the ways professional work blocks rather than fosters proximity. It is also a job for citizens to hold professionals and professionalized public institutions to higher, more participatory, standards. These are really big jobs, as we will see, because our institutions often do not want us to be too involved in the work they do for us.

2

Institutions as Fields of Action

*[I]nstitutions are socially organized forms of paying atten-
tion . . . although they can also, unfortunately, be socially
organized forms of distraction.*
—ROBERT BELLAH ET AL.

Bearing Up, Taking On, Throwing Over, and Reconstructing

The United States has had a long history of democratic eruptions, but it is worth noting how constructive many have been. Americans have borne up with systemic injustice, threats to the common good, and entrenched hierarchies, but then taken them on, thrown them over, and then built or reconstructed institutions to serve as preventatives.

Eighteenth-century revolutionaries remade colonial institutions they had come to detest. They moved capitols to the centers of their states, refashioned legislative bodies so a broader swath of the population could stand for office, trimmed executive powers, and ensconced the participatory institution of the jury at the heart of the least participatory branch of government. Nineteenth-century abolitionists took on and threw over the wretched institution of slavery that had brutalized slaves and dehumanized slave-owners and passive onlookers alike. Late-nineteenth- and early-twentieth-century populists and progressives fundamentally reshaped public institutions held in sway by corporate interests, using initiative and recall devices. Later in the twentieth century, the civil rights and women's movements similarly worked from within the system through reconstructive legal challenges.

My point is not to present a Whig historical sketch that glosses over conflict, fissures in the body politic, or chronic, persistent institutional failures, especially with respect to subgroups. Nor do I think any of our previous epochs was a civic Eden—a golden age of participation. Rather, I want to stress that twenty-first century Americans are no less fed up with their institutions.[1]

We know from this history of bearing up, taking on, and throwing over that even institutions propped up by ancient assumptions are vulnerable to change. Yet, though there are eruptions of dissent today, beneath this surface protest we lack a constructive spirit of rebuilding. We seem stymied by how concrete our institutions are, how amorphous the public can be, how dependent we are on faceless systems for ordering our social world and helping us become the people we wish to be. As we saw in the last chapter, we struggle to find the conceptual language for conceiving institutional change; influential schools of democratic theory either turn away from the bricks and mortar world of institutions or bypass it altogether.[2] There is a civic lethargy afoot in the land, and our institutions like it that way.

The Two Faces of Institutions

Like most kids growing up in the 1970s, I quickly became aware of institutional power and savvy to the ways it could create and destroy. In grade school, many of us deeply admired the previous generation's scientific achievements such as the moon landing, while viscerally fearing and resenting others, such as the sophisticated weapons and game theory models bringing the prospect of nuclear annihilation ever closer. As undergraduates, we studied the Robbers Cave and Stanford Prison social psychology experiments, which showed how institutional labels—in-group or out-group, guard or prisoner—could strongly influence how students no different from us could generate solidarity while treating others as enemies and subhumans.

Institutions bring out our best and our worst. They help us form and maintain intimate attachments, organize and apply scientific knowledge, produce and deliver goods and services, and enact the very rules we live by. Yes, they may be complex, but this complexity helps us grow as individuals and as a society. Think of playing first violin on a Brandenburg Concerto without an orchestra, a music education, and many years of patterned practice. Or try to imagine interstate highways, stable financial markets, or widely accessible schools and universities without the public funding, regulation, and focused planning made possible by government.

Yet institutions can also be profoundly negative influences in our lives. Twenty-five years ago, Robert Bellah and his coauthors argued that American institutions were seriously dysfunctional. "Democracy means paying attention," they wrote, and American democracy had not been paying much attention—to the way government, work, and even family structures had become "corrupt; means have wrongly been turned into ends," in particular the ends of narrow economic success and individual fulfillment.[3] When they are saturated by values of the marketplace, or by patriarchy or racism or homophobia, our families, jobs, and laws will be correspondingly affected. Institutions focus our attention, sometimes on the wrong things:

> We live in and through institutions. The nature of the institutions we both inhabit and transform has much to do with our capacity to sustain attention. We could even say that institutions are socially organized forms of paying attention or attending, although they can also, unfortunately, be socially organized forms of distraction.[4]

Bellah et al.'s argument is a deep critique of the cognitive, moral, and civic barriers institutions pose to the realization of American democracy: "Because we have let too much of our lives be determined by processes 'going on over our heads,' we have settled for easy measures that have distracted us from what needs to be attended to and cared for."[5] Beneath the surface of democratic politics—which can erupt as it is in our time in waves of dissent and protest—there is an institutional layer constraining our ability to focus and work effectively together on major problems. If we care about improving our democracy, this layer, in which many of us spend much of our working lives, should be a primary focus: how can we find ways to share professionalized tasks with outsiders, listen to them, and engage their concerns, and how can we encourage professionals on the inside to listen and work with us? This strategy of institutional co-production and collaboration may be more effective in the long-term than a more "fugitive" politics of resistance.

To see something as an institution is to recognize that it is more than an instrument that serves a fixed purpose but instead is a semiautonomous domain with a history and an organizational density that make it difficult for those outside the domain—or in one corner of it rather than another—to understand. Moreover, an institution works on us even as we work within it and through it; institutions are significant forces in our lives.

Sociologists and others who study institutions think of them as stable arrangements that guide our actions and comport with communal values.[6] Institutions emerge to accomplish tasks that would be difficult to manage in a more inchoate or ad hoc fashion, such as to help us cope with the grief and loss and conflicts that are part of human social life as well as our needs for nurturing and healing and respect, but they do so in a way that inevitably reflects the values and commitments of the social order in which they are embedded.[7] Marriage and family life, the practice of medicine, the meting out of justice, and the education of the next generation, among many other undertakings, are all institutionalized, and they all reflect social norms regarding proper relationships, roles, and interactions; they exist to make certain actions easier and others harder.

Even though most institutions are public to some degree, in that they are socially embedded, we can differentiate some as *public institutions* when they produce non-divisible common goods such as public safety, are supported by public revenues, and are managed by people held publicly accountable. Private institutions, by contrast, produce private goods—as when a private security force protects only certain individuals, paid for and held accountable primarily to a subgroup such as a homeowners' association. The public nature of an institution places a special burden on it to install and heed public procedures of accountability that can determine whether the institution is, in fact, infused with widely shared values.

However, the special burden tends to be rather lightly felt. Sociological research on institutions shows how the rules and offices that impose useful regularity can also conflict with intended values. One famous study of democratic organizations found that institutional delegation of authority and division of labor led to concentrations of power that violated the groups' value commitments to equality. "Who says organization," Robert Michels chillingly wrote, "says oligarchy."[8] He thought these power-concentrating tendencies strong enough to call them "iron laws," although contemporary scholars dispute their strength and universality.[9] Yet even if they are not iron or ever-present, the propensities of institutions to align themselves toward internal rather than external purposes are powerful and common enough to pose problems.

Even more troublesome than the ways institutions violate their own core values are the barriers they place on thought. While it is true that institutions are social creations, it is also true that they powerfully shape how we think about them, and indeed who we are. This is not a matter of corrupt institutions or power-hungry elites; it is standard operating practice. "How can we possibly think of ourselves in society," writes Mary Douglas, "except by using the classifications established in our institutions?"[10] "They fix processes that are essentially dynamic, they hide their influence, and they rouse our emotions to a standardized pitch on standardized issues."[11] This is just what institutions are for: they label, classify, and order. They think for us. As Douglas puts it, "The instituted community blocks personal curiosity, organizes public memory, and heroically imposes certainty on uncertainty."[12] Our dependence on institutions to tell us when we are "smart," and "capable," and "educated," for example, helps explain some of our anxiety about getting into exactly the best college and securing the right kind of degree; the better the college we are in, the "smarter," the more "capable," and the better "educated" we must, inevitably, be. Institutions, in fact, provide social validation and meaning for people—a student once told me he wanted to be a lawyer so he could wear a suit to work every day. Yet we need to be more reflective about the ways our institutions produce barriers to how we see and experience other people. Wear the suit, be validated, but also try your best to notice how your institutional world invalidates and clothes marginalized others in very different kinds of outfits.

Especially important is how institutions can think for us in ways that extract what are really complex moral choices about complicated human beings and replace them with sheer process, thus deflecting concern for others. They can strip away aspects of human beings that make a person familiar, replacing them with other features that make it harder for bureaucrats and officials to recognize and act on a responsibility to safeguard people's welfare inside and outside the institution. Zygmunt Bauman has called this the "management of morality," occurring in modern institutions through the "social production of distance, which either annuls or weakens the pressure of moral responsibility," through the "substitution of technical for moral responsibility, which effectively conceals the moral significance of the action," and through "the technology of segregation and separation, which promotes indifference to the plight of the Other which otherwise would be subject to moral evaluation and morally motivated response."[13]

The institutional management of morality occurs quite straightforwardly and without a moment's notice in professionalized domains such as health, education, criminal justice, and government. In criminal justice, for example, people are distanced from their law-abiding fellow citizens and treated in a technical rather than moral fashion as soon as they are suspects, a process that continues as defendants are given a case number and finally compelled to wear orange jumpsuits and shackles in court. Such management of morality is normal for institutions that handle a large volume of human business: complex men and women turn into clearances, caseloads, and dockets. The very "language in which things happen to them," writes Bauman, "safeguards its referents from ethical evaluation."[14] These linguistic and material forces of separation are even stronger with respect to human beings accused of harming others. By the very accusation, they have already become a candidate for expulsion from the warm "circle of proximity where moral responsibility rules supreme."[15]

Repellent Institutions

In addition to doing our thinking for us and shaping how we perceive those they have a hold of, many institutions repel public examination and participation in three distinct ways. Staying with the example of criminal justice, consider how much of the work being done is physically removed from both the lay public and any official not directly involved with trying a defendant, caring for a prisoner, or guiding a parolee. Erving Goffman called prisons "total institutions" because they are separate and complete worlds for those inside; communication and interaction with those outside, indeed even visibility, are all tightly circumscribed and controlled.[16] The work of administering criminal justice—handling the content of probation orders, among other tasks— is normally conducted outside the public byways. Mandated courses on life skills, anger management, and the like are often held in buildings and sites lacking any exterior signs communicating that something relevant to the public is happening inside. Court professionals' reliance on plea bargaining means very few criminal cases ever go to public trial. Even when there are trials, their hierarchical management leads many jurors to find them bureaucratic and oddly disempowering.[17]

Second, criminal justice institutions repel public examination and participation because of their sheer complexity. As Lucia Zedner points out, the common phrase "criminal justice system" should be resisted "on the grounds that this label masks its plural, disparate, even chaotic, character."[18] What is really a "series of largely independent organizations with differing cultures, professional ethos, and practices" is not easy even for practitioners to understand, much less members of the lay public.[19] In his critique of the kind of structured distraction that permitted America's steep rise in incarceration, William Stuntz indicates how a many-handed decision-making process thwarted the assessment of responsibility:

> Where state and local officials alike were responsible for rising levels
> of imprisonment, neither was truly responsible. Prosecutors sent more
> and more defendants to state prisons in part because state legislators
> kept building more prison cells. . . . For their part, the legislators kept
> adding to their state's stock of prison beds because local prosecutors
> kept sending defendants to state prisons: if they're coming, you
> must build it. Neither set of officials fully controlled the process by
> which those prison beds were made and filled, so neither was able to
> slow or reverse that process. And the voters with the largest stake in

that process—chiefly African American residents of high-crime city neighborhoods—had the smallest voice in the relevant decisions.[20]

Even the officials and professionals involved in specific decisions at one level cannot be said to plan, intend, or even fully comprehend the cumulative institutional consequences of their actions.

Third, and most subtly, criminal justice institutions repel public awareness and involvement because they perform and characterize tasks in ways that neutralize the public's role. Critics advocating a more "restorative" approach have argued that criminal justice institutions "steal conflicts" and have "a monopoly on justice."[21] These are dramatic ways of saying something quite uncontroversial, namely, that most public institutions have something to prove: that they are the experts in providing healthcare, justice, information gathering, or education, thus justifying why each respective institution deserves to expand its budget and authority to tackle social problems. In fact, institutions are constantly in competition with non-institutional modes of accomplishing the same goals and thus have a tendency to characterize social problems in ways they can manage. State institutions in particular, by monopolizing coercive force, can make it seem that they are the difference between order and chaos, yet this is an illusion. Informal social control is far more important than the formal coercive measures criminal justice institutions deliver, and yet our public discourse—influenced by the ways our institutions think for us—construes courts, prisons, and probation officers as the active agents and families, neighborhoods, and civil associations as passive recipients of crime control benefits produced by institutions.[22]

Yet perhaps we should just shruggingly acknowledge the ways institutions think and act for us as simply part of modern life. We are surrounded, after all, by complex and quasi-autonomous systems such as financial markets, so why is it surprising or troubling that public institutions are also complex and quasi-autonomous?

Here we must draw a normative distinction between institutions that require greater public steering and those that do not. Some institutions have clearly defined and uncontroversial objectives, the pursuit of which is easily monitored. Civil engineering agencies that plan and build highways, sewers, or airports may not always require regular and significant public engagement. Other institutions are charged with tasks that do not have discernible, long-lasting, negative effects on human lives. The Bureau of Weights and Measures no doubt influences how we count and calculate, but it does not appear to hold much risk of impairing people's lives. By contrast, it should be obvious that institutions such as criminal justice, healthcare, and education lack clearly defined, uncontroversial, and easily monitored objectives, and at the same time pose enormous risks for impairing human development if their work is done poorly or unfairly.

Ankle Monitor

Consider the story of Savina Sauceda who, while in nursing school at the age of twenty-three, was arrested for delivering a felony quantity of cocaine. Sauceda had not even incurred a traffic ticket before this arrest, but she had started selling drugs to pay off her school and credit card debts. She received a five-year prison sentence. But the Illinois department of corrections, housing forty-five thousand prisoners with an additional thirty thousand on parole at a cost of over a billion dollars a year, had become a target for budget cuts during the depths of the Great Recession. Here is how the story was framed on National Public Radio, known for its reflective and progressive reporting:

> With budget crises to solve, many states have decided that reducing their prison populations is a good way to save money. Illinois is one example. Under its new early release program, as many as 1,000 non-violent offenders will be able to finish their sentences at home or at other locations approved by prison officials. Corrections costs are typically a major component of state budgets. So as burgeoning prison populations blow holes through those budgets, more states are looking to cut costs and change policies.[23]

The narrative relates a wise economic decision under straitened budgetary circumstances to release a nonviolent offender with no prior criminal record after serving a year in prison. Although this is a story of an institution becoming more moderate, it is also strangely depressing. Absent is any discussion of the normative goodness or badness of the fact that a nonviolent offender with no criminal record and on track for employability served a year in prison and could have served up to five years. Absent, too, is any locus of normative judgment. Could this woman really have received the following sentence: "One to five years, depending on the state budget?" Where was the collective mind that had decided that five years was right at time-1 and then changed its mind at time-2? Could we speak to that mind, interview it to ask if saving state dollars was a justifiable reason for the difference between Sauceda being in or out of prison? This story disturbs because it indicates a missing moral force—an absentee public, a "we" for which a punishment such as Sauceda's makes sense. How could a person's fate be so capriciously determined by institutional imperatives only loosely coupled to the very set of normative values that justify the institution?

We are not thinking when we sentence Sauceda to one to five years, and we are still not thinking when we send her back home with an electronic ankle monitor after serving only one year. Someone else is not thinking either. Rather, the thinking and the responsibility for thinking are diffuse and incredibly difficult to trace, to get a hold of. This is because criminal justice institutions are both public and repellent to the public.

Citizen Responsibility for Public Institutions

Although they are complex and quasi-autonomous, public institutions cannot function without taxpayer support. They often operate under the oversight of managers selected by officials elected in free, competitive elections, and they purport to deliver goods such as education, healthcare, and public safety. Although they frequently resist or repel public responsibility, they are nevertheless the public's responsibility. To put it plainly, the public needs to better own up to the work being done by their institutions. Wherever core values are plural and contested, wherever neglectful or uncaring policies and practices have severe consequences, and wherever an institution depends upon the public to function, the work is our responsibility. If we are to have public institutions at all, we must hold ourselves accountable for what they do and for the reasons behind their actions.

My view differs somewhat from similar arguments distinguishing legitimate from illegitimate institutions. Legitimacy arguments valorize consent: subjects of rules or laws should have a concrete and not merely symbolic role in authorizing them and should understand what they must obey.[24] Yet I think being part of a good institution means more than making sure its rules and laws serve your own interests. I favor a broader conception of collective self-government: good institutions allow you to influence and help steer the powers to which you contribute and which speak and operate in your name, but they also call you to account for how they treat other people not like you, and to stand up, when needed to address discriminatory or repressive or otherwise inhumane practices. When institutions distance the work of education, healthcare, and criminal justice from lay citizens, we may become unknowing supporters of rules or laws that affect people differently—some well, others poorly; some fairly, others unfairly. Think of how like sleepwalkers most Americans went about their daily routines for decades while our country became what Nils Christie called the "world champion of incarceration," by locking up a greater percentage of our citizens than any other democracy, with glaring racial disparities, brutal conditions, and staggeringly long sentences for some.[25] While such a lack of awareness, reinforced by and indeed produced by modern institutions, can harm our personal interests, what troubles me is the lack of concern for others it permits. I think the problem is not merely the individual risks posed by the public institutions we choose not to steer, but the difficulties such a diffuse and quasi-autonomous system presents in our holding each other accountable for our laws and how they affect others who are not like us.

Institutionally fostered public ignorance and civic lethargy turns citizen-beneficiaries into collaborationists. We must, as laypeople, become more inquisitive and more alert to what our institutions do and how they do it; we must, as professionals and professionals in training, be more creative about aligning them to communities while constructing access points for citizen agency and platforms for citizens to think together in close proximity. Otherwise our misaligned institutions will continue operating under their proximity deficits and serve as powerful counter-democratic forces in the background of all our social and political reform efforts.

The sort of democracy we are discussing here is not anti-institution—320 million people live in the United States, after all. It simply requires a more central place for human contact and particularized responsibility. We must rationally disorganize our way back into our institutions, and innovative democratic professionals can help us learn how. In Donnan Stoicovy's democratic school, for example, there are routine opportunities for students to solve administrative problems, develop ongoing rules, and shape the curriculum. Education, to some degree, is not delivered to them; they are co-producing it. Their educational institutions are not thinking and acting for them, but with them.

Nurturing more responsible public institutions is different than just getting more people engaged, and it is not about fixing ignorant and uncaring citizens. It is about building access points, forging alignment, fostering proximity, and infusing citizen agency at critical junctures throughout all of our public institutions. The kind of citizen–professional collaborations democratic professionals aim to foster directly address and reform the kinds of counter-democratic tendencies and asocial structures that reinforce callousness and make social problems difficult to handle.

Participatory Democracy Inside
An Institution-Focused Theory

Participatory democracy is the theoretical perspective most congenial to the issues I have raised about institutions, and it appears, in varying forms, as the normative core of democratic professional motivations. Yet there is much scholarly skepticism about participatory democracy: for some it seems flaky and self-involved and for others overly optimistic about the willingness of citizens to be more engaged. It is often dismissed by canonical treatments of democratic theory as naïve—lacking the critical bite of more pessimistic theories and insufficiently disciplined by the kinds of rules developed by proceduralists.[26]

Participatory democrats draw attention to the significant flaws of modern governments, but they are not pessimistic about civic agency. Instead, they attempt to theorize what should motivate citizens to occupy a more active role in the political culture broadly understood. Though sharing many of the concerns of proceduralists, participatory democrats place an emphasis on power-sharing and agency and are much more skeptical about representation. This makes them worried about the ways theorists are modeling actual participation, and in particular their use of deliberative forums as microcosms of the general public.

Contemporary participatory democratic scholars such as Carole Pateman, Francesca Polletta, and Donatella della Porta argue that mini-publics and other deliberative experiments have failed to promote or connect with effective grassroots citizen agency.[27] Most deliberative experiments, participatory democrats point out, seem to be temporary, top-down affairs that do little to empower ordinary citizens or to produce lasting public critiques or challenges to entrenched social and economic inequalities that structure citizen agency. Surveys of politically engaged citizens, for example, who have also participated in deliberative experiments, or have encountered them in their activist work, reveal high levels of ambivalence and some distrust; despite the surface neutrality of deliberative forum engineering, most activists view forums warily as risky top-down efforts.[28] For participatory democrats, deliberative forums operate at a hermetically sealed distance from community organizing efforts at the local level and other forms of activism at the national and international levels.

Participatory democrats belong to an extended lineage of thinkers who distrust representative institutions while knowing, realistically, that they need to work in and through them. The Anti-Federalists in the American constitutional debates, for example, rejected James Madison's argument that elite bodies—if structured in the right ways—can protect individual rights and pursue the people's long-term interests better than the people themselves convened for that purpose. Anti-Federalist critics argued vehemently against Madison that the common people's interests could never be adequately represented by elites; so they supported shorter terms of office, smaller electoral districts, and a more decentralized system overall. They were ardent defenders of the jury system precisely because it valued citizen agency and called on citizens to be "centinels and guardians of each other."[29] Note that the Anti-Federalists were not simply oppositional, as they offered constructive institutional modifications in response: bolstering the jury, for example, was needed to rebalance the relationship between professional judges and lay jurors and, more generally, between the principles of representation and participation.

Modern participatory democrats are less concerned about the venues available for non-elite citizens to express their policy interests and make their voices heard as the laws of the land are written and enforced. They are more worried about a different kind of loss that results from representation: the relaxation of generalized responsibility for what the state does or fails to do to others that accompanies representation's division of political labor. This kind of civic responsibility is frequently criticized as either utopian or overly communitarian and intrusive, and therefore participatory democracy is sometimes too easily dismissed as impossible or archaic.[30] There are reasons to think it is neither, however.

Standard accounts of participatory democracy have two primary components. The first is an argument that participation in collective decisions and public action helps people so involved become better in some way: more respectful of others, more competent at public decision-making, more reflective about the larger society, and more aware of their own self-interests and better able to effectuate them. The "key hypothesis," writes Arnold Kaufman, faculty advisor to Students for a Democratic Society activists in the early 1960s and the originator of the term "participatory democracy," is "that in advanced industrial societies participation is, in balance, beneficial because of the contribution it makes to individual personal development."[31] Participatory democracy's "main justifying function," according to Kaufman, who drew closely from Mill, is "the contribution it can make to the development of human powers of thought, feeling, and action."[32]

The second element of the theory is the argument that collective discussion and decision should extend into domains commonly thought apolitical, such as workplaces, families, and institutions such as universities, hospitals, and clinics. While never exempted from formal legal regulation, such domains are traditionally seen as governed by personal or professional norms. Participatory democrats argue that these are the sites in which most people spend much of their lives, where they are judged adequate or inadequate, where they learn who they are and what they are good at doing—in short, where human development takes place. The Students for a Democratic Society wrote of "a yearning to believe there is an alternative to the present, that something *can* be done to change circumstances in the school, the workplaces, the bureaucracies, the government."[33]

A less-discussed third component of participatory democracy is responsibility. Kaufman's "development of thought, feeling, and action," though couched in the language of *self*-development, was clearly meant to encompass other people and society at large. Echoing Tocqueville's and Mill's suggestion that participation presses individuals to consider others' interests, Kaufman writes "only when men acquire direct responsibility for a certain range of decisions that social imagination breaks through its parochial barriers and envisages larger possibilities."[34] Responsibility is intertwined with self-development, for Kaufman: "The main justifying function of participation is development of man's essential powers—inducing human dignity and respect, and making men responsible by developing their powers of deliberate action."[35]

Homing in on the meaning of responsibility for participatory democrats, the function it plays in their arguments, and the ways it worked in their practices helps us tighten up what are otherwise rather loose normative commitments to general human development and broad participation. These loose commitments make participatory democratic thought look either idealistic and archaic, on the one hand, or solipsistic and self-involved, on the other. Instead, I think responsibility for self, others, and the common public world is the primary normative orientation of participatory democracy, and it makes it a more robust political theory than it is usually given credit for being.

The classic activist proclamation of participatory democratic goals is the "Port Huron Statement," written mostly by Tom Hayden of the Students for a Democratic Society. The main lines of the argument are well known, so I want to emphasize how participation is construed in this essay as not just good for the self, for others, and for the social, economic, and political domains that currently discourage it, but as morally required by the irresponsibility of institutions and actors of conventional politics and the mainstream business world. Participation is not urged in a mushy utopian sense, but as a concrete remedy to specific harms and wrongs that are either misrecognized or rationalized by elite representatives and managers and underactive members of the general public.

The essay begins with self-critique. The middle-class complacency with American institutions and values in which these student activists grew up could not withstand assault from real world events:

> Our comfort was penetrated by events too troubling to dismiss. First, the permeating and victimizing fact of human degradation, symbolized by the Southern struggle against racial bigotry, compelled most of us from silence to activism. Second, the enclosing fact of the Cold War, symbolized by the presence of the Bomb, brought awareness that we ourselves, and our friends, and millions of abstract "others" ... might die at any time. We might deliberately ignore, or avoid, or fail to feel all other human problems, but not these two, for these were too immediate and crushing in their impact, too challenging in the demand that we as individuals take the responsibility for encounter and resolution.[36]

For Hayden and the SDS, participation is required. It is not the result of a happy-go-lucky impulse for self-development or aimless do-gooding, but called for by specific harms, dangers, and injustices produced by conventional institutions and actors. Once the generalized *doxic* complacency of middle-class life—the unfelt pressure to "ignore, or avoid, or fail to feel ... human problems"—is punctured by massive institutional failures to live up to American values, other failures begin to come to awareness: a wide range of "complicated and disturbing paradoxes" such as the hollowness of American commitment to equality evident in Southern segregation, Northern urban poverty, and the misery and meaninglessness of much industrial work; equally paradoxical is the deeply held belief in the principle of government by consent in the face of an "apathetic and manipulated" democratic system.

It is essential to notice that these failures to live up to core values and principles articulated in founding documents, manifest in the most important political settlements in the country's history, and ensconced in textbook descriptions of American government were not the result of conventional institutions and actors behaving badly or anomalously, but the result of the system working *normally*. The proper functioning of American representative democracy had led to dramatically immoral and hypocritical outcomes: avoidable threats and harms to well-being and dignity. Worse still than their own irresponsibility, the complexity of representative institutions and their inherent distance from citizen action had led to widespread irresponsibility in the form of apathy among the public.

This issue of responsibility for a social, economic, and political system that is held up by the beliefs, actions, and resources of the people, that is not effectively steered by them, and that is failing to live up to fundamental values shared by them is at the center of participatory democratic practice as well as theory. As student activist Gabriel Breton argued in 1962:

> The recognition of the right of every member in the society to participate in the affairs of society is not based merely on some attitude of democratic fair play, but on the knowledge that every individual bears the burden of the problems of society and of mankind, and that his own responsibility as a moral agent commits him to work towards their solution.[37]

Responsibility is what propels participatory democrats' deep distrust of the divisions of labor in conventional politics and formal government institutions: these divisions may be efficient, but they endanger our ability to be a good society as defined by uncontroversial and traditional values.

Representation of others' interests, indeed, the very idea of "leadership," were suspect for participatory democrats. The leadership style of some left-liberal civil rights organizations was seen as corrosive to the extent it let citizens off the moral hook to organize themselves, to recognize and assert their own interests. A chief organizer for the Student Nonviolent Coordinating Committee's work during Freedom Summer 1964, Robert Moses, "always intensely distrusted leaders who prevent the growth of a capacity for responsibility in others: he [was] famous for sitting in the back of meetings, avoiding speeches, and when obliged to speak standing in his place and asking questions."[38] Participatory democratic leadership was deliberately horizontal to encourage widespread not hierarchical responsibility. Moses took the idea that everyone had the capacity to be a leader so much to heart that he changed his surname to Parris to deflect the idea developing in the media that he was the chief moral leader of the movement.[39]

Critics of participatory democratic thought note how it blurs the distinction between self-development and social improvement and seems to encourage or at least tolerate self-involvement and the trivial politicization of everyday life. But this criticism loses much of its force once we sharpen our understanding of *what* concretely was being opposed and *what* the activists were responding to with *moral disgust*: institutions run by elites claiming to represent public interests actually promoting policy that wasted or deformed human lives. Institutions that actively corrode human development turn seemingly unaffected beneficiaries into witnesses and collaborationists; they send a moral signal to do something.

The normative force of participatory democratic theory comes from its critique of the ways institutions think for us, act for us, and, in the process dehumanize us. These human creations are shielding us from inhumane consequences, shielding us from others' suffering, shielding us from what we might do about it. The theory targets fundamental flaws in the contemporary social, political, and economic worlds we inhabit that need to be addressed before any other reforms are possible. It gives priority to civic agency over deliberation for this reason; to act is to begin to see; action is not more important than reflection, of course, just more foundational as it is action that brings us in contact with others.

One can argue, of course, that even with this standard the fuzziness returns: everything, including issues as abstract as rules formulated by the Bureau of Weights and Measures, must influence human development somehow. A participatory democrat can respond that some institutions require more democratic control, more public responsibility simply because they pose the greatest threats to human development. To return to our main example in this chapter, criminal justice institutions deserve greater scrutiny, awareness, and popular involvement. Not only is the outcome some form of punishment that should be used as sparingly as possible because of its negative effects—dehumanization, shame, and physical suffering, for example—but also because the current system, at least in the United States, is so marked by both racial and socioeconomic bias, as poor, urban minority men fill the prisons at wildly disproportionate rates.

So widespread alert and responsible participation is called for, required, in fact, in institutions that have the potential for great harm to human development. To be healthy the political culture must foster the kind of general responsibility that is needed to adequately steer and check such institutions. Insulated representatives, even those advised by the most thoughtful and humane experts and professionals, cannot take up this responsibility for the general public.

Democratic Professionals and Participatory Innovation

For a number of years now I have met and interviewed democratic professionals working in a range of fields and institutions. They are quietly, subtly, and without much academic attention or media fanfare reconstructing schools, clinics, city governments, criminal justice programs, and many other established practices all around us every day. What this has meant, in practice, is that democratic professionals *rationally disorganize* their domains: they are alert to the ways their organizations and institutions reflexively disempower the agency and trivialize the knowledge of laypeople; they consider how normatively central—not minor or symbolic—tasks can be altered so that laypeople can take part or become more aware; and they establish regular self-sustaining opportunities for load-bearing participation and dialogue.

The kind of participatory innovation that matters does more than simply encourage more citizen involvement; we are looking for certain qualities not just quantities. Greater quantities of participation on terms already fixed by institutions means little if we are concerned with transforming their repellent aspects. Too often, for example, participatory community policing reforms are conceived programmatically as the community helping the police with "their" job of keeping the public safe.[40] This, in my view, fails the test of participatory democracy, though it could be redeemed by deepening departmental commitments to real power-sharing. What we will view as participatory innovations are instances in which institutions open up to citizens and think and act with and through them. The word some scholars use to criticize policing reform—"responsibilize"—is an awkward but fitting name for the quality we are looking for: democratic innovations that have value are those that actually responsibilize people to take up substantive tasks in the institutional world all around.[41] Democratic schools allow students to think for themselves about education and to play a role in adjusting institutions accordingly. Democratic criminal justice institutions call on citizens to think about punishment, to do punishment and conflict resolution and rehabilitation. Democratic city management calls on citizens to think about social problems as co-producers of solutions, not as clients.

I have been asking democratic professionals across the United States the following sorts of questions to get to these qualitative features of participatory innovation:

(1) How have you repaired or created spaces of proximity and collaboration in your organizations? How have you, as an innovative public administrator, for example, brought citizens into reflective contact with each other to do substantive, non-symbolic work?

(2) How has your democratic practice shifted or shared responsibility for the goals of your organization? How have you, as a democratic criminal justice

practitioner, for example, managed to incorporate nonprofessionals into your decision-making while ensuring competence and accountability?

(3) How have you released the capacities of those throughout your operational hierarchy and of those affected by your organization but not employed by it? How have you, as a democratic teacher or principal, for example, broken the traditional barriers that distance you from students in the service of institutional order?

(4) What have you created that will outlast your career? Have you shifted institutional habits so that the inefficiencies of lay participation are recognized as costs worth paying in order to enjoy collective or long-term benefits? Have you successfully and durably trained the next generation of democratic practitioners who will take up similar roles in your organization?

These questions are informed by key elements of the pessimistic and proceduralist strands of democratic theory noted in the last chapter, but they are guided by a more grounded and participatory democratic theory alert to the ways everyday makers and other active agents are called to make a difference today. They presume that contemporary citizens have not done enough yet to repair and remodel what remains of the participatory infra-structure we inherited. They ask what practitioners are creating today that will foster the forms of proximity that can generate the attunement to others and public responsibility lacking in nearly every school, hospital, and prison in our country, and in the administrative offices that touch most of the other domains of social life.

Inside some very beige buildings along some very normal streets are re-markable people breathing new life into American democracy. Let's get to know them.

3

Democratic Innovation in K-12 Education

. . . schools will be the dangerous outposts of a humane civilization.

—JOHN DEWEY

AS STRESSED IN the theoretical framework developed in the previous chapters, democratic professionalism is a mode of democratic change that operates inside and alongside institutions. It is not an ideology, but a set of habits, attitudes, and practices. Democratic professionals encourage talk and deliberation but, crucially, they also foster a way of being together, of co-owning certain shared problems, of working on things together. Though they may belong to practitioner networks and engage in ongoing streams of print, online, and face-to-face dialogue, democratic professionals do not make up a typical social movement. They are not seeking change by organizing and mobilizing large swaths of activists and putting pressure on power-holders to make law or policy that then can impact their professional domains. Rather, they are making changes in their domains piece by piece, practice by practice: renovating, reconstructing, and making things. The things democratic professionals in K-12 education are making are democratic schools.

Context and Motivations

Democratic professionalism has not been championed by teachers' professional associations and is not part of teacher training programs at universities.[1] Moreover, despite the teaching establishment's loud concern about youth civic disengagement in the last generation, efforts to create more democratic schools are, in scholar and advocate Dana Mitra's words, strongly "counter normative." "While they encourage young people to participate in community service, schools tend to fall short on preparing youth to develop and lead such activities. Thus schools tend to teach students to be passive participants in a democracy rather than leaders."[2] Civic engagement and service learning are mainstream now in the nation's schools, but such programs are normally embedded in astonishingly antidemocratic institutions that remain hierarchical, rule-bound, and inegalitarian. Mitra writes of "the inertia of conscious and unconscious beliefs and procedures that tend to suppress the voices of students and their value in contributing to more effective decisionmaking in schools."[3]

Mainstream schooling is antidemocratic most powerfully in the attitudes adults have toward children. As Vanessa Gray, a reform-minded principal at Forest Grove Community School in Oregon, notes, "many adults just don't see kids as equals—as people they can learn things from."[4] Inequality in adult-child relations in primary education is so obvious we do not even notice it, and it is true that some kinds of inequality are warranted by the responsibility unrelated adults have for minors during the school day. Yet the assumption that youth are clients of education provided by adults rather than the active agents of their own education is common and pernicious. If the public world that is the school is rigidly ordered and commanded from on high—perhaps even constrained by powerful forces beyond the reaches of the principal's or superintendent's office—untouchable and unmovable by those most affected by it, then the hidden curriculum being fostered is that some of the most important problems facing society cannot be solved by lay citizens. At the very same time they are being encouraged to be of service, to learn about branches of government, to embrace core political values, most students across the country are excluded, fundamentally, from reflectively shaping the social environment that is their school.

The depth and breadth of antidemocratic attitudes, norms, and practices in American schools can be shocking. Democratic professional reformer Deborah Meier reflects on her first experiences working in a typical school:

> I observed firsthand what democracy is *not* like! From the perspectives of both a would-be teacher and students, school life was as far from what a democratic ethos is all about as one could concoct—except perhaps for modern prisons. The army allows for more camaraderie than schools, and even the General Motors assembly line is more sociable and respectful of human dignity.[5]
>
> I remember the first and most striking reaction I had to Chicago's South Side public schools—that they were (and probably still are) the

most disrespectful environments, even for adults, that I had ever experienced. There is a special smell, taste, and feel to many elementary schools of petty humiliation imposed to remind teachers and children of who's the boss.[6]

From "rules and norms we didn't understand," to "tone of voice" and "rank ordering"—even "lining up by size or alphabet for very young children can seem demeaning"—there is, at best, a careless sort of "benign dictatorship" that characterizes most schools.[7]

Despite such a challenging environment, democratic practitioners in this field have formed inchoate networks—such as the National League of Democratic Schools and the Institute for Democratic Education in America (IDEA). The League was founded by educational reformer John Goodlad in 2004, to recognize and promote democratic schools, defined as "learning communit[ies] characterized by a commitment to democratic goals and values . . . evident in the curriculum, school policies, practices, and organizational structures."[8] Members of the League hold meetings at national education conferences and communicate via informal networks and regular newsletters. Founded by activist Scott Nine, IDEA seeks to mobilize "action to advance meaningful learning and build a more just and sustainable democracy" by leading tours of democratic schools, helping communicate and foster democratic practices, and supporting democratic education conferences.[9]

Reformers have found significant success in big and small schools, among varying socioeconomic populations, across urban, suburban, and rural communities. Many practical ideas are incubated in the nation's alternative schools, especially the highly participatory Sudbury Schools, also known as "Free Schools." The Sudbury Valley School, founded in 1968 in Framingham, Massachusetts, is run by direct democracy under strict egalitarian norms. The two dozen or so private Sudbury schools across the country promote institutional cultures in which students have a strong steering role in what and how they study, with as little as possible in the curriculum predetermined or standardized. Yet, democratic professionalism is alive too in a number of public schools that are well ensconced in traditional mainstream educational systems. I have focused my interviews and research on public school teachers and principals in different regions of the United States who are committed to democratic schools. While still far from common, innovative democratic practice has deep roots in American education and has found a home in all kinds of schools.

Historically linked to the century-long wave of progressive education reform and to student power efforts in the 1960s, contemporary
democratic professionals in K-12 education are motivated by three main
factors: *professional identity, academic engagement,* and *civic education.* All
three are seen by reformers as under threat in an era in which many curricular decisions are decided far from the local context in state and national
government offices.

Professional Identity

Bitter complaints about "teaching to the test" and the pejorative use of the
phrase "high-stakes testing" are common among teachers in the wake of No
Child Left Behind and subsequent policy developments under the Obama
administration, but in my conversations and background research I was
struck by how the centralization of education policy at the state and federal
levels and the greater use of standardized testing was experienced as an assault on teacher professionalism. "I feel like an appliance," one democratic
teacher said; instead of using her professional judgment in her classroom,
she is encouraged to conform to a preprogrammed set of messages.[10] We find
ourselves "becoming technicians," writes democratic principal Dianne Suiter,
"trained to deliver state and nationally determined curricular objectives in an
attempt to create student 'products' who can quickly recall and dispense an
alarming quantity of memorized information, which by its very nature must
be delivered at an equally alarming pace to afford the necessary coverage of
material."[11] "Few policymakers observe that such testing is an emblematic case
of technocratic experts seeking to engineer outcomes and practices in ways
that displace the agency of the educators, students, and communities that
know their children best."[12]

Reflecting on his own experience teaching in three different settings—
from Teach for America, to a private school, to an urban charter school—
democratic professional Paul McCormick observes that in each case "the
content I taught was already decided. My job was dependent upon student test
data and value-added algorithms foreign to even my principal." Everywhere
he turned he saw "hierarchical management, arrogant attitudes, and a fundamental lack of investment among everyone involved."[13]

As John Goodlad—an intellectual guide for many reformers—puts it,
what is lacking in the contemporary school is "the necessary autonomy of
agency that good teaching requires. Thinking has been taken out of the schoolhouse just as it has been taken out of the workplace beyond."[14] Democratic

professional teachers find the pressures that are "deskilling" them abhorrent, resist "the redefinition of their work as the implementation of others' ideas and plans," and want to exercise their "right to help create their own programs for professional growth based on their perceptions of problems and issues in their classrooms, schools, and professional lives."[15]

Teaching professionals are caught in a bind growing ever tighter by relations of distrust between schools and the public, between students and teachers, and between teachers and administrators on site and off. "We don't trust teachers' judgment, so we constrain their choices. Nor do we trust principals, parents, or local school boards. We don't trust the public school system as a whole, so we allow those furthest removed from the schoolhouse to dictate policy."[16] Measures meant to evaluate teachers' performance, such as standardized tests, and materials meant to establish curricular baselines, such as mandated textbooks, can also produce distance between teachers and their subjects and their students that breeds even more distrust and disengagement. This vicious circle of distrust of the teaching profession has created an institutional environment nobody wants to be part of: "We've invented schools that present at best a caricature of what the kids need in order to grow up to be effective citizens, skillful team members, tenacious and ingenious thinkers, or truth seekers. They sit, largely passively, through one after another different subject matter in no special order of relevance, directed by people they can't imagine becoming, much less would like to become."[17]

Academic Engagement

Academic engagement is another motivation for professionals seeking to create more democratic schools. Students who are able to participate more in the shaping of the curriculum and the everyday practice of their schools have greater opportunities to identify with their school. The more students feel a part of a school community the more connected they are with the pedagogical side as well. "When we present students with opportunities to be involved in school improvement work," reflects democratic principal Nelson Beaudoin, "when we give them a say in the decisions that affect them, we increase their sense of belonging and accomplishment."[18] In his high school, Beaudoin says, "my students will see themselves as volunteers rather than prisoners—young people with the skills and knowledge needed to sustain our democracy." Democratic practices are often advocated as ways of connecting with alienated students. A school where students feel like they are contributing—to the process, to the school itself, to their and others' education—is a school where students feel at home, have a sense of belonging, and want to show up for classes. Research has shown that democratic schools positively impact students' competence as well by developing their ability to critique their environment and increasing their problem-solving, group facilitation, public speaking, and social skills.[19]

Consider a story I call "Ironman," with personal names altered to preserve anonymity. Osborne, a 9th-grader at Forest Grove Community School, was the last student one would expect to come forward on his own accord at the yearly student-run talent show, with a large number of students, staff members, and parents in attendance. He had more than enough to worry about at an age when young people are painfully aware of what their peers think of them. Osborne had significant mental and physical impairments. He was loud, sometimes spat when he talked, moved in a jerky way, and could be hard to be around. Even the casual observer would recognize that he had severe difficulties. But one day he announced that he wanted to sing Black Sabbath's "Iron Man" for the talent show. So he did, getting up, midway through the event, to sing a cappella every verse and chorus of one of Heavy Metal's most bombastic, monotonous, least inspired, and slowest-paced songs.

Has he lost his mind?
Can he see or is he blind?
Can he walk at all?
Or if he moves will he fall?
Is he alive or dead?
Has he thoughts within his head?
We'll just pass him there,
Why should we even care?
He was turned to steel.
In the great magnetic field.
When he traveled time,
For the future of mankind.
Nobody wants him,
He just stares at the world.

When he was finished, the whole audience clapped, and one of Osborne's teachers from an earlier grade approached the school principal with tears in his eyes. "That was the most beautiful moment I have ever seen. I cannot believe that in an auditorium of over 200 kids I watched the faces of all these kids and did not see one kid who laughed or made fun or exchanged a look with another classmate. I think that is incredible." Osborne himself was glowing, thrilled to have been able to perform in front of everyone.[20]

Connecting with students on their own terms can also, counterintuitively, strengthen a teacher's sense of professionalism, as a Madison, Wisconsin, democratic teacher notes:

> When young people asked, "Why do we have to learn this?" . . . I was sometimes not really sure how to answer them. The students were frustrated and so was I. As a result of these less-than-satisfying experiences as a teacher (as well as some during my own school years), I began talking to colleagues and friends, trying to create another view of school. We talked of designing school experiences that involve students in all aspects of classroom life, including curriculum planning.[21]

Democratic teaching thus emerges as true professionalism—indeed as a savior of professionalism—not only because it expresses workplace autonomy, but also because it is more precisely attuned to the needs of those it aims to benefit than state-mandated, prefabricated instruction.

Civic Education

Civic education, the third main motivation, is thought of in robust terms: not just more teaching related to government or public policy, but as a qualitative immersion in concrete social problem-solving starting as early as kindergarten. This is to "nurture and develop the attributes of democratic citizenship in our future neighbors," notes democratic principal George Wood. "These schools are laboratories where democracy is experienced," he continues, "not museums where it is just observed."[22] Democratic professional teachers and principals hope that students will "learn by doing" and that the power-sharing, horizontal relationships pervading their institutions will have an influence inside and out. "All the habits of mind and work that go into democratic institutional life," argues Deborah Meier, "must be practiced in our schools until they truly become habits—so deeply a part of us that in times of stress we fall back on them rather than abandon them in search of a great leader or father figure, or retreat into the private isolation of our private interests."[23] Advocates see democratic schools as more than models, but as real-time remedies to pervasive counter-democratic tendencies in mainstream education and other social and political institutions.

Reformers view contemporary schools as not conducive for forming a democratic public. Indeed, they see schools as expressive of and often contributing to the continued fragmentation of political society. Reformers are frequently sensitive to social justice issues and perceive how their schools transmit rather than challenge existing socioeconomic disparities in the surrounding community. "Democratic educators seek not simply to lessen the harshness of social inequities in school," write Apple and Beane, "but to change the conditions that create them. For this reason, they tie their understanding of undemocratic practices inside the school to larger conditions on the outside."[24] Stand-alone civic engagement curricular modules and add-on service learning programs, even if mandated for all students, are insufficient to break this circuit. The school itself must be an environment where, despite differences in ability, vast gaps between well- and poorly-off students, people learn to respect what others can contribute to the life we have in common. "I have come to realize that the most important thing I can do to prepare students for their lives as adults in our shared democratic world is to help them talk with, and listen to, each other," notes democratic teacher Vale Hartley, after pointing out how so many adults lack the willingness and ability to "assume the responsibility of governance."[25] "The opportunity to lead others," writes Dianne Suiter, "to have their ideas heard, and to make a difference in the community is far less likely for some of these students. With every lost opportunity comes an increased risk that some will never even try to become full members of society."[26]

While traditional models of civic education assume functioning social and government institutions outside the school that young people will be able to successfully contribute to, upon graduation, if they are suitably informed and prepared, the idea of civic education in democratic schools assumes a surrounding dysfunctional environment that reproduces hierarchy and social distance. A surprising amalgamation of optimism and pessimism comes together in the idea that democratic schools are a kind of rescue institution for American democracy. "For many children and their families schools are one of the few institutions that can provide the experience of membership in an enlarged common community."[27] Yet the idea of the democratic school as the embodiment of democracy in an undemocratic time is laid out in very practical ways, stressing horizontal relationships, task-sharing collaboration, and proximity: "In schools," says

Meier, "kids sit down next to their classmates, whoever they are. Parents proudly come together at school concerts, weep together at graduations, and congregate in times of crisis at public hearings and PTA meetings. Public schools therefore offer opportunities for a sense of community otherwise sorely missing, for putting faces and names to people we might otherwise see as mere statistics or categories."[28] As a student puts it, "We know we need to work together. Even if we don't like one another we get over that because we want to work together."[29]

One should not conclude that democratic schools are schools intending to shape students into activists, to imbue a specific political ideology. The point, as reformers put it, is more subtle: it is to see "how far schools could go in creating a deeply internalized attraction to democratic ideals, habits, and practices" in a time when most major institutions are doing the opposite.[30] Though they may use terms such as "nurture," "develop," "learn," "practice," and "experience" at times, which imply young people are incomplete citizens without the civic education schools provide, this suggested asymmetry is offset by the collaborative nature of the environment: everyone, including the adults, has something to learn about thinking and acting democratically. Adults, indeed, have a lot to learn from kids about their specific, diverse, and grounded experience. "Rather than focusing on 'becoming' citizens," note Mitra and Serriere, the point is to "focus on and value the contributions that young people can make in the present day. Civic education, from this perspective, is not only about developing skills, knowledge, and attitudes for future participation, but also recognizes and values children as citizens in their own right, with standpoint knowledge about their current social and political communities."[31]

Democratic Schools

So what, exactly, is a democratic school? As teacher Jim Strickland puts it, using very Deweyan language, "democratic schools are schools that use democratic means to advance democratic ends."[32] They involve students much more thoroughly than mainstream schools in curriculum design, teaching, and institutional governance. Reformers are well aware of what David Mathews has called "democracy lite," merely token or symbolic efforts; they want student involvement in their schools to be significant, lasting, and empowering.[33] Two main components of democratic schools, then, are *democratic modes of teaching* and *participatory institutional structures* that make a meaningful difference in the educational experience.

Democratic Teaching

Democratic teaching, at its most fundamental, involves students in the co-production of knowledge. "A democratic curriculum," write Apple and Beane, "invites young people to shed the passive role of knowledge consumers and assume the active role of 'meaning makers.'"[34] This is a systematic and careful process that goes far beyond having spontaneous conversations in class about what is happening in students' lives: "it is directed toward intelligent and reflective consideration of problems, events, and issues that arise in the course of our collective lives. A democratic curriculum involves continuous opportunities to explore such issues, to imagine responses to problems, and to act upon those responses."[35] In a democratic school in Madison, Wisconsin, students were asked "to identify questions and concerns they have about self and world" and these became the basis of class work. Students asked: "How did my skin color come about? What will happen to me after I die? When will gang violence ever stop? Why are some kids popular?" These and other questions became the focus of small-group work, with links drawn between those having to do with the self and those having to do with the world. With traditional disciplinary knowledge in the background, students in schools like these become part of a community of learners where what they bring into school—in the form of questions, experience, and frames of reference—is a valued part of the collective project.

Consider a narrative I call "Seeds," documented by democratic first grade teacher Kerry Salazar:

> NATE: The seeds are afraid of birds, mice and deer. My seed's house has stoves below it and if they hit the secret alarm the pulley will bring the stoves up so it's too hot and no one can get in.
>
> CALVIN: I'm digging a burrow for my seed. No one can get him if he's in his burrow.

At the beginning of the year the children in Opal 1 had many experiences wondering about seeds. They brought in seeds from home, counted seeds, drew seeds, made seed characters and began to play with their seeds as they imagined what their seeds would need. To them, it seemed, their seeds were so vulnerable, and much of their time playing with their seeds was spent dreaming up ways to protect them. Our job as teachers during this time is to be paying particularly close attention to what the children are wondering about—even when their wondering doesn't sound like questions. We ask ourselves: Where are the ideas that are complex and meaningful enough to capture and sustain this particular group of children's attention and sense of wonder over time?

A small group of children observed and explored the beautiful seeds in a pomegranate.

LIAM: The seed skin protects the seeds—to keep the insides in just like us! Here was an idea we could spend some time wondering about. Do we need protection too? Are people and seeds alike? Do they need the same things? What do we need protection from? Certainly not animals trying to eat us. But what then? What does protection look like? Is it the same for all of us?

TEACHER: How are seeds and people alike?

ZEHREN: We're kind of like the fruit and our heart on the inside is like the seed.

LIAM: Our heart is like the pit!

LUCIUS: We're like the plant. Our heads are like the pit and our neck is like the stem.

CALVIN: So, what's the seed?

LUCIUS: Our brain.

BRIDGER: Our legs are the roots.

ZEHREN: We both grow bigger and bigger and older and older.

NATE: When you die you might plant love and stuff. When you die your body just grows invisible love flowers. It's just planting love.

CALVIN: The bulb or seed is like the heart. The seed that gets planted. Like the heart makes you. If you didn't have a heart you'd die and if the corn didn't have a seed it'd die.

Again, the words of the children lead us to more possibilities, to wonder, to explore, to deepen our understanding of ourselves and each other. Here are some of the questions that will move us forward: What helps us to grow? Do we have to come out of our shells? What does that mean? What do you need to feel safe enough to come out of your shell? How do we protect our hearts? How do we protect the hearts of others? How do we protect our community?[36]

At democratic first grade teacher Kerry Salazar's school, Opal School, in Portland, "curriculum is a process of negotiation between children's ideas and curiosities, adult resources, Oregon standards, and issues and events happening in the world."

Democratic teachers seek to create an environment that reveals the value of inquiry and cultivates habits of reflective thought for students and teachers alike. Deborah Meier tells an apt story we can call "Darnell and the Rock":

> I was so certain that the distinction between living and nonliving was a "simple" idea. I chose the most obvious: a rock and our gerbil. I figured I'd leave the gray areas for later. But five-year-old Darnell insists on making it difficult. Is he putting us on? "Rocks change too, and rocks move." He reminds me that on our trip to Central Park I described how the rocks had come down with the glaciers, and how they change shape over time. He won over some of the kids. They reproduce, said one: little rocks break off from big ones. I feel I'm losing the argument. So much for my neat chart.[37]

Reflecting on this exchange, she wonders, "How can we show kids that it is precisely in such ideas that important discoveries are made, rather than closing the conversation off with an 'explanation.'"[38]

While science and math curricula are often some of the most rigidly imposed directives coming from state and district departments of education, democratic teaching makes headway in the receptivity of classrooms to student-led inquiry precisely by modeling scientific open-mindedness, as Kerry Salazar's conversation about seeds and the story of Darnell and the Rock illustrate. Democratic schools often strive to connect classroom topics and skills to pressing problems faced by neighborhoods and communities surrounding the school. Hands-on learning about water quality, conservation, and urban development, for example, shows the relevance of otherwise abstract-seeming analytical tools of natural and social scientists. Even when course materials in math and science have to come from "on top," democratic teaching encourages "bottom up" questioning, collaborative projects in applied math and science, and self-directed inquiry sparked by personal interests.

Democratic teachers can also incorporate student interests even more fundamentally in the shaping of their courses. As social studies teacher Paul McCormick relates, "I did not anticipate teaching a class with the performing arts teacher about the Broadway musical *Hamilton*, until the students suggested this was a viable class and I actually learned about the musical's content and how perfect it would be to blend into a combined social studies and performing arts class."[39] The professional power of course design, when shared, can produce something of greater relevance and interest for all involved. In McCormick's 5th-12th grade school, for example, nearly all courses, with the exception of the relatively traditional math curriculum, "are first vetted for student interest, while at the same time balanced with teacher interest and expertise. As a result, course offerings are a combination of the passions of both teachers and students."[40] Though power-sharing might appear as a threat to teaching professionalism, and in more hierarchical contexts quite easily could be, in democratic schools committed to cultivating habits of reflective thought power-sharing expresses a kind of mutual attraction for the learning process. Teachers are not owners of the school as laboratory; they are working alongside students, guiding, taking on suggestions for further research questions, and considering in all seriousness, even seemingly "wrong" categorizations—Darnell's living rock—that could lead to important conversations about the ways scientists need to think to understand the complex systems of a dynamic world.[41]

Along with efforts that encourage co-production of knowledge through student-led inquiry, democratic teachers often find other ways of task- and power-sharing in their classrooms. Some have older children mentor or tutor younger ones in subjects such as reading and writing. Others place children in positions of power over social ordering—helping other kids work responsibly together—and even share pedagogical authority. The experience in one Wisconsin school is both counterintuitive and instructive, as it shows how older students can grow into responsibility:

> a fourth-grade teacher was having trouble with her students' behavior when they went on walking field trips to the nearby Milwaukee River. The kids would get too close to certain parts of the river. This behavior changed dramatically when she paired her students with first graders. The older students outdid themselves to make sure that the younger students didn't go too near the water.[42]

Other schools use peer-evaluation committees to assess student work, as when high school seniors help judge required end-of-year projects. In Deborah Meier's school, students are part of graduation panels modeled after PhD committees: "a panel of reviewers—faculty and family members, students, and external community people or professionals—make the final judgment." The student panel members are full participants with the adults in evaluating student portfolios and presentations; they "ask questions, probe for strengths and weaknesses," alongside the adult members and they together reach a collective judgment about the work.[43] "A deep way students are involved in learning," says school reformer Helen Beattie, "can be their co-creation of assessments or defining proficiency or mastery goals and the path to that end."[44]

In addition, democratic teachers foster core values—of free individual expression and capacity development, respect for self and others, and equal treatment—through routines, such as regular circle meetings guided by strong deliberative norms, that call for participation and dialogue. "We sit in a circle," says Dianne Suiter, "so that everyone is equal and we all are equally included visually with each other." "All are expected to show respect to others . . . And the rules apply to all—even the adults!"[45]

Participatory Structures

The democratic structures put in place by innovative professionals include reconstructed versions of traditional participatory school practices such as student government and school newspapers, but they include new forms as well such as regular student-led town hall forums. To make student government more inclusive and less of a popularity contest, democratic principal Beaudoin replaced traditional elections with a process where students could become members of the main advisory body if they attended three meetings. The student-led advisory body in Beaudoin's school was also given significant responsibility: "What areas in the realm of school-based decisions need to be off limits to students? I cannot think of one. Decisions about curriculum, decisions about the school environment, even important safety considerations such as emergency lockdown procedures can benefit from student input."[46]

In democratic principal Joe Greenberg's 6-12th grade school, students lead an all school town hall meeting once a week and serve on administrative bodies such as a maintenance committee for issues related to the school building and grounds and two tiers of courts for handling student offenses. Democratic principal Jon Downs' 5-12th grade school has a thirty-minute "Democracy in Action" period blocked off every day either before or after lunch to be used by students to meet in advisory committees, convene all school meetings, and collaborate on other relevant projects. In democratic principal Donnan Stoicovy's K-5 school, the 5th graders run all school groups every Tuesday afternoon for 45 minutes. "The kids know when they're fifth graders that this is part of their responsibility to our school—to be the leaders of all school meetings. I see kids who normally wouldn't get up, get up in front of the whole school. They blow me away when they stand up there!"[47] Democratic schools may also convene constitutional conventions so students can come up with governing documents on their own and agree upon school values, norms, and codes of conduct. These shared tasks go beyond symbolic deference to students by an otherwise adult-run organization: student-influenced dress codes and cell phone policies go into effect, student preferences are tallied in staff hiring decisions, and student perspectives on grading systems are integrated into changing methods; these and many other conventionally adult practices are shaped by working collaboratively with young people.

Other ground-level democratic practices are common in these schools. Student-directed mediation, for example, often takes place to resolve conflicts or draw attention to problems between students. At Trillium, a public K-12 charter school in Portland, at least half of the students have been involved in mediation, according to one well-informed 5th grader. A mediation mat is rolled out and the main parties involved stand on spaces marked out for specific roles: "Report," what you view as the problem to be solved, then "Listen," to what the other person has to say, "Brainstorm Solutions," and finally, "Agreement," where the parties stand together in the middle of the mat. At Westside Village Magnet School, one student having a problem with another is to cool off, then talk it over with the other student—sharing how she feels about what happened and listening in return. If this does not resolve the issue, the student can come to a mediator and say, "I need help solving a problem." Adults will also ask, "Do you need to go to mediation?" Mediation begins with finding a quiet place, preferably with a round table. The mediator asks the participants to make four agreements: "Agree to solve the problem; tell the truth; use active listening; search for a win/win solution." The first person is asked to state what happened and how it made her feel, which is then paraphrased by the mediator. Then the other party is asked the same thing. When everyone is done describing the problem, the mediator asks whether a "win/win" solution can be found. The school has a chart that can be used to suggest such possibilities as "talk it out," "compromise," "say 'sorry,'" "make a peace offering," and "put it off."[48]

In many subtle and almost imperceptible ways, too, democratic schools encourage horizontal communication among students, teachers, and administrators: this, most simply, through the expressed attitudes of respect, attention, and welcome given to student contributions by those with formal authority.[49] It is common for administrative directors of democratic schools to balk at norms and titles and symbols that prop up centralized, concentrated authority. By helping prepare and serve lunch in the school cafeteria every day Principal Downs disrupts conventions about work hierarchy and leadership in his school. Stoicovy calls herself "lead learner" rather than "principal" to stress the collaborative nature of the

organizational mission. Suiter rejects "traditional hierarchical styles of op-
eration" and "top-down procedures," in favor of collaborative "shared leadership" in which the principal is "located more at the center of our work,
rather than at the top."[50]

Consider a story we can call "Democracy at Lunch: The Salad Girls."
Three 5th-grade girls in Park Forest Elementary School wanted to eat salad
for lunch but could not. The pre-made salads the cafeteria sold came with
meat and cheese and were off limits for lactose intolerant Anika, Muslim
and vegetarian Sana, and Orthodox Christian Olivia, who could not eat
meat on Wednesdays and Fridays during Lent. Up against cafeteria workers
who protested that they were not authorized to serve the salad in any other
form, the girls asked their teacher and principal what to do. They were told
to gather data on how many other students shared their views about the pre-
made salad and to seek out ways of solving the problem. The girls then prepared a brief speech and PowerPoint presentation, which they delivered at
the weekly all-school gathering held at Park Forest to inform the rest of the
school's 450 students. Following the presentation, the girls went to each classroom and conducted simple agree or disagree opinion polls on whether the
salad options should be changed at lunch. They found that 90 percent of their
fellow students agreed with them on the need for a broader choice of salads.

With the data in hand, the salad girls approached the head of the cafeteria to brainstorm a solution. Mrs. M. explained that she was bound by US
Department of Agriculture protein and calcium requirements in her lunch
offerings, so she could not offer the kind of flexibility the girls desired. In
addition, lunch had to be efficient, and a salad bar would slow down the
pace of students moving through the line. Unbowed by this bureaucratic
but not unreasonable response, the salad girls kept researching alternatives
by conducting interviews and looking into possible solutions online. After
the girls presented this second round of research, the principal suggested that
they meet with the district-level cafeteria manager, Ms. Y. Like Mrs. M., Ms.
Y. was clear about the USDA requirements school cafeterias had to heed.
However, she was willing to look for alternatives with the girls. Finally, they
agreed that Park Forest would become a "trial school" for having three salad
options at lunch: the usual, with meat and cheese, one with meat but not
cheese, and one with cheese but no meat.

At the next all school gathering the salad girls proudly announced that the
cafeteria had changed its menu. Nevertheless, they continued to research the
issue they had spent so much time on, collecting data on how many students
chose the new salad options.[51]

In conversations with democratic educators and during visits to their schools numerous examples arose of students coming forward with projects done for the school on their own initiative. At Westside Village Magnet School the week I visited, for instance, a girl dropped off a shoebox of money in the principal's office. Unbeknownst to the staff, she had been knitting crafts and selling them on behalf of the school. At Forest Grove, students painted an ocean-themed mural to brighten up a previously seedy, graffiti-ridden alleyway near two community gardens they manage.[52] As important, students in democratic schools are more comfortable speaking out about practices they think are unfair and proposing solutions of their own. A note written to democratic principal Dianne Suiter implicitly critiquing her distribution of privileged bleacher seating to certain grades illustrates this point:

Dear Dr. Suiter,
A lot of kids think that the Intermediate should sit on the bleachers. The little kids are smaller and can sit longer in any position. Plus, we are the oldest kids in the school, so we should be the ones to sit in the bleachers.

We think that we can prove that we can sit in the bleachers quietly. Please give us a chance.

Sincerely,
(almost all of the students in that class signed their name)[53]

It is easy for adults—who are at liberty to freely offer advice and opinions to other adults and especially to children—to miss how constrained young people normally are in their ability to offer critical feedback to the older, taller, and bigger people who are always in charge. Horizontal participatory structures placing adults in positions of mutual sharing, listening, and working with children foster a culture of open critical dialogue that can be created in no other way.

The Future of Democratic Schools
Barriers to Growth

What are the barriers innovative professionals face as they try to build democratic schools? This research indicates that external stakeholders can sometimes hinder growth: school board members, superintendents, and parents may press for very narrow outcomes such as job-readiness. As an antidote, democratic teachers and principals can go a long way by involving parents and community members early and often in the founding of new schools or the shaping of new operating frameworks. As Deborah Meier puts it, "Democracy requires acknowledging power, its delegation and distribution. Schools need to also." Her school openly distributes power between internal (staff and student) stakeholders, and external (parent and community) stakeholders. The principal is responsible to a board of governors made up of "equal numbers of parent and staff representatives, along with an equal number of community members chosen by parents and staff, plus two senior students."[54]

Internal stakeholders may also find democratic teaching and structures difficult. Even those committed to horizontal and collaborative decision-making processes report a "democratic fatigue" that results when "staff, students, and parents engage in long-running deliberation of ideas and initiatives within their school."[55] Tensions can emerge, too, among people with varying levels of commitment. Democratic principals often find it hard to work with teachers who have a top-down mindset—not uncommon given the marginalized status of democratic professionalism within teacher-training programs. Principal Greenberg in Ithaca, for example, has hired former students from his school in order to ensure its commitment to democratic practices and teaching.[56] Counterintuitively, some democratic principals, such as Donnan Stoicovy have to enforce democratic norms by fiat, establishing "non-negotiable components of fostering civic engagement" and trusting that once these are in place "some teachers will eventually 'get it.' "[57] From the standpoint of teachers, on the other hand, Cristina Alfaro has noted how critically important a supportive principal was to her democratic work; she could only get her democratic teacher-training program underway in schools where principals cared about these values.[58]

Being a democratic teacher is not easy, either. Power-sharing in the classroom challenges the authority of knowledge, experience, and office many teachers come to rely upon in their work. Neophyte teachers, or those struggling in their craft because of scarce resources, limited training, or difficult classroom environments, may cling to traditional hierarchical roles. My interviews and background research indicate that teachers who gravitate toward nondemocratic practice may do so as a way of anchoring their shaky authority in the classroom. Horizontal relations in the classroom also take time: it takes time to have a meandering conversation about seeds; it takes time to explore with Darnell all the ways rocks do and do not resemble living beings. If reformers are right that schools must resemble laboratories in which what is being examined all the time, every day, is the education process itself, this can be experienced as a very demanding set of expectations. Stimulating, maybe, for students and teachers alike, but also tiring; small wonder that the easier path of prefabricated curricula, lesson plans, worksheets, course materials, and fill-in-the-bubble tests is so often taken.

When I ask democratic teachers and principals why there are not more schools like theirs, their responses tend to reflect a complex set of external constraints. Education policymakers in state and federal government want specific results delivered by schools: improved standardized test scores and higher graduation rates. They want predictability and control; they want particular kinds of data about school performance on tap when they request it. They want teachers to measure up to certain specified qualifications. A successful 12-year veteran teacher at Westside Village Magnet School had to be recertified and was in danger of losing his position because he lacked one of the newly established qualifications. Because democratic schools are less hierarchical and favor a group-oriented power structure rather than the principal-led top-down organization, they are less predictable and "rational" in the traditional Weberian sense. A story we can call "Bells All the Time" provides a humorous but telling illustration:

> My secretary interrupted our meeting three times today. A man from the Board insisted on knowing our "bell schedule." I told her to tell him (a) we had no bells and (b) there were three schools in the building and each had different schedules. He wouldn't be put off. So I told her to tell him they went off "every hour on the hour." He was satisfied.[59]

Their rational disorganization is good for democracy, but makes it more difficult to comport with official requests. They are also, according to a number of reformers I interviewed, less accustomed to selling themselves and promoting their work in the conventional terms favored in the contemporary school reform debate.

Importantly, one thing that is not a barrier is money. It does not cost more to be democratic in all the ways that count. Student-inquiry-oriented Opal School is a learning paradise filled with the tools and supplies children need to explore the natural world on their own terms, but these are the simplest materials imaginable and are often brought in by parents and students themselves. Democratic teachers and principals do not have higher salaries than mainstream colleagues and their buildings are no better or worse. Though it is true that time is money and democratic practices take more time, in no other way that I discovered are democratic schools less economically efficient.

Overt versus Covert Democracy

Democratic schools sometimes wear the label proudly. Democratic principal Greenberg's school website, for example, makes a very public declaration:

> [We are] a democratically-run learning community where students share with the staff in the day-to-day operation of the school. Each student participates in these three areas of school and self-governance:
>
> Family Group—a small advising and support group of 1–2 staff members and 12–14 students meeting twice per week working on curricular and cultural issues.
>
> Committee—a group meeting twice per week working in decision-making groups (e.g. Alternative Community Court, Agenda Committee) or action-oriented groups (e.g. Eco-action, Maintenance, LACS Café) to help run the school.
>
> All School Meeting—a once per week "Town Meeting" led by Agenda Committee members where the entire LACS community discusses and decides pertinent all-school issues, most-often generated by student and staff proposals.[60]

Stoicovy's school includes democratic themes in its mission statements, calling itself "A caring community of learners connecting our learning spaces to the world outside," and dedicating itself to "relevance, authenticity, involvement, and voice." "Providing a laboratory to live and learn democracy" is thus tightly integrated into the public purposes of the school.[61]

In other schools, however, democratic professionalism proceeds covertly. Rather than announcing themselves through explicitly democratic language, such schools, even if led by reform-minded principals and staffed by teachers who are enthusiastic democratic professionals, appear from the outside as mainstream in character. Democratic principal Robyn Davis stressed that, though she had a very supportive superintendent, many parents of students in her school would balk at an explicitly democratic curriculum, worrying that it would turn their children into lifelong Democrats! So she speaks publicly about common core themes such as habits of mind and about getting young people to talk and engage in school while keeping the democratic nature of her school submerged.[62] "Student voice" initiatives and "youth-adult partnerships" are two other ways reform-minded professionals democratize their schools by stealth.

A good example of covert democratic professionalism is the ten-year-old Youth and Adults Transforming School Together (YATST) program in Vermont involving 27 schools across the state.[63] YATST schools put together teams of adults and students who meet regularly during the school week for two years to conduct action research on ways to improve their institutions; after this initial period, YATST often becomes a standing committee at schools and endures over time. YATST teams conduct focus groups, surveys, and other forms of data gathering, which they then analyze and present to larger groups in their school to form deliberative action plans. For example, after data gathering, analysis, and deliberation one group of YATST students, "in order to increase shared responsibility in learning . . . have partnered with faculty to develop a credit-bearing option for students to become Classroom Assistants, providing instructional roles in classrooms. They recently received school-board approval to pilot this initiative."[64]

An illustration of covert democracy in practice comes from Hazen Union High School, in Hardwick, Vermont, which has been affiliated with YATST for eight years. A few years ago a science teacher approached the principal with a problem. Every year all the regular academic routines come to a halt for the week that students take traditional mid-year exams. The teacher questioned: Are these tests worth it? Wouldn't students get more out of a regular academic week? Is there another way to assess student achievement? The principal called on the YATST team—made up of fourteen students and one advisor—to facilitate a school-wide conversation.

The team decided to use a "reverse fishbowl"—participants seated around an inner circle share their thoughts on a list of questions posed by a youth facilitator while those in the outer circle listen. When the speakers are done, they trade seats with the listeners who move into the inner circle to talk about their responses to the same questions and their reactions to the first round of comments. The team came up with three main questions for the facilitator to ask the "fish":

1) When you hear the words "mid-year exam" what comes immediately to mind?
2) Do mid-year exams accurately measure your learning? Why or why not?
3) What suggestions do you have for alternative means to effectively measure your learning?

In the first round, nine students sat in the inner circle. They felt that, while exams seem important for getting into college, they are imperfect measurements of knowledge or aptitude. Furthermore, exams are stressful and hard to prepare for, and the memorized information is often quickly forgotten. They wondered if the school could find a way to evaluate student learning that is more tightly integrated into the subject matter. When the faculty took the inner circle, they echoed the students' concerns, describing similar experiences during their own high school years. They shared doubts about how well exams capture what their classes are achieving. Many were frustrated with the format and the process. One teacher summed up the group's sentiments: "If so many of us feel this way, why do we still do this?"

Later that same week, the principal and the faculty leadership team began working out changes to the school examination process. Teachers at Hazen Union now use a wider range of tools to evaluate what their students are learning, including project-based assessments, reflective writing assignments, and other measures.

While everything more overt advocates of democratic schools desire is evident in this program if one looks closely enough—highly sophisticated co-production of knowledge, power- and task-sharing, non-hierarchical ways of communicating and participating, and commitments to deep transformative change are all clearly present—"democracy" appears only rarely in the YATST core materials.

Resources for Long Term Sustainability and Expansion

Democratic professionals overcome the barriers to their work one problem at a time. Apart from context-specific tactics of covert and overt democratic strategies, three kinds of resources are available for the long-term sustainability of democratic teaching and participatory institutional structures. The first is the training and reproduction of other people committed to this work. A common phrase I heard in talking with K-12 democratic professionals about the sustainability of their schools is "relationship building." Democratic principals and teachers seek out those like-minded individuals who want to participate in the co-ownership of an educational environment, who want something more out of their career than a paid staff position. Kieran Connolly, democratic principal of Trillium School, talked of a teacher who wanted him to evaluate her by surprise visits to her classroom. Instead, he suggested a working relationship where she would come to him when something was not working and say, "Here is the problem, how do we solve this—together?"[65] Opal School has ongoing institutional relationships with teacher-training programs at schools such as Butler University in Indiana that stress student-led classrooms and active learning; students in programs such as these are welcomed in to Opal as week-long visitors and even as assistant teachers. Teachers can thus "learn by doing" as they circulate through democratic schools.

Another resource for sustainability and expansion is the codification of craft practices. Though many would resist the idea of a democratic school template as counter-democratic, it is evident that democratic professionals are learning from one another in loose networks. In conferences, in workshops, and in online discussions, they share stories that illustrate what practices are working or not working. This is the kind of craft knowledge that, thankfully, cannot be put into standardized form even if that was desired. Yet the *process* of transmitting and absorbing craft knowledge could be formalized: teacher-training programs committed to a more democratic professionalism could demand that students on this track spend a certain number of hours at democratic schools in their region. In turn, democratic teachers and principals could decide which schools are the most appropriate venues, supplying an updated list every year to the training programs.[66]

A third resource comes from outside schools in the form of nongovernmental or civil association assistance. Democratic teaching and participatory structures have been sparked and sustained by community organizations and other bodies with a stake in reform.[67] Such groups can provide ideas, support people, and small pockets of funding that shore up internal efforts. YATST in Vermont, for example, is part of a nonprofit organization, UP for Learning, which offers versatile, open-ended templates for collective work and has fostered a growing network of reform-minded teachers, principals, and students.[68] While external groups must be careful, for the sake of ground-level support and "ownership" of a program, not to drive a process that is best steered from students and teachers inside schools, they can provide critical assistance at the outset of reform efforts, and during periods of stagnation, and they can also be on hand as "a coach on the side" whenever needed.[69]

Democratic professionals in K-12 education are making essential changes, one school at a time. Though what they are doing is not at the forefront of reform discourse in American education policy and is not the subject of teacher training programs in universities, these democratic teachers and principals offer a compelling picture of what real democratic education looks like. It is hard to see how we can repair our nonparticipatory and repellent social and political institutions without the kinds of schools these democratic professionals are building. As important as their large-scale consequences is their immanent value: democratic schools are good for the students in them. Their practices and structures allow free spaces, encourage forms of proximity that close social distances, and provide many opportunities for young people to express their voices and to work together with others as partners in what is ideally a life-long educational project.

4

Democratic Innovation
in Criminal Justice

*American criminal law's historical development has borne
no relation to any plausible normative theory—unless
"more" counts as a normative theory.*
—WILLIAM STUNTZ

CRIMINAL JUSTICE INSTITUTIONS are both more and less impervious to democratic innovation than they seem at first glance. They are more resistant, despite the inherently public nature of their task, because of the many ways they repel public awareness and involvement, which we discussed in Chapter 2: the background institutional environment of policing, prosecution, plea bargaining, adjudication, imprisonment, and probation is largely nontransparent, hierarchical, and non-participatory. Nevertheless, as we also discussed, the criminal justice system is not really a "system" and therefore contains different professional cultures, and multiple access points for innovation, as well as normative, political, and economic motivations for improvement. Pressures to reform stem from deep concerns about the fairness, efficacy, and sustainability of mass incarceration and from heightened protests regarding conventional policing. Moreover, criminal justice happens in many rooms: at the police department, in the prosecutor's office, and in the courtroom, of course, but also the Watts mosque we visited in the Preface where a gang truce was settled; the elementary schools we encountered in the last chapter, where everyday conflicts are worked on by students themselves; and many other quasi-formal sites in which tensions, problems, and frictions can receive the hearing and settlement they deserve.

Context and Motivations

Motivations for innovative reform are present on the inside and outside of mainstream institutions, and there's a palpable sense of urgency about racially biased patterns of policing, adjudicating, and punishing.

Nothing Works

The last quarter century has been a dismal time to be a criminal justice professional. Some scholars have called this the "nothing works" period, an era of exhaustion with the two major prevailing theories undergirding their institutions.[1] The first, rehabilitation, also known as penal welfarism, understood punishment as a means to correct behavioral and thinking patterns that lead to harmful acts; it held sway until the 1960s. Facing liberal challengers on one flank concerned about indefinite sentences and widely varying penalties for the same offense depending on the corrigibility of the offender and, on the other, conservative critics irked by the moral vacuity of a clinical paradigm for understanding violent acts, rehabilitation gave way to the retributive, or just deserts, model with rigid sentencing guidelines that pegged sentences to the seriousness of the offense. Yet neither approach succeeded in achieving the goal of humane public safety with the minimum of coercion. Crime rates continued to rise and so did rates of incarceration.

From a relatively lenient status quo, at least in the North, the United States rapidly moved in the mid-1970s to a condition of "hyperincarceration."[2] In 1972, for example, 64 out of every 100,000 citizens in the State of New York were incarcerated, a ratio consistent with the previous hundred years; by 2000 this figure had risen to 383/100,000, in keeping with the even higher national trend over the same thirty-year period.[3] By 2007 the country housed 2.4 million inmates, with 1 out of every 198 Americans behind bars.[4] Adding probation and parole to these figures, by 2007, 1 out of every 31 adults in the United States was under some kind of correctional control.[5]

This trend began, to some extent, in response to increasing urban crime rates. It continued, however, even after crime rates tapered off in the early 1980s and then again in the 1990s, by tougher sentences for nonviolent crimes such as drug trafficking and by procedurally fair but substantively harsh mandatory minimum laws taking away judicial discretion.[6] Also relevant to penal expansion is the "business" of incarceration, once called the "prison industrial complex," involving for-profit prison corporations' political influence, guard union support for mandatory minimum sentencing, and the economic benefits of prison construction for impoverished rural areas.[7] By the end of the century, the United States was leading the world in incarceration, with a higher percentage of its citizens in prison than any other country.[8]

While the effects of crime on victims and communities are significant, punishment itself brings about severe consequences. Most evident with the penalty of incarceration, they include shame, dehumanization, feelings of inferiority, and physical suffering. Many of these consequences are experienced to some degree too by the spouses, partners, children, and other close relatives of the incarcerated.[9] In most states in the United States, those convicted of a felony lose their right to vote: in 48 states for the duration of the imprisonment, in 36 for the duration of the probation or parole period, and in 13 for life.[10] Economic consequences can also be significant, as prisoners' families struggle with lost wages during incarceration and severely impaired incomes afterward. Bruce Western and Becky Pettit report that "serving time in prison was associated with a 40 percent reduction in earnings and with reduced job tenure, reduced hourly wages, and higher unemployment."[11]

Alongside these negative effects are the equally troubling racial and socioeconomic biases of the current system. As Wacquant has pointed out, it may be misleading to call the current rise in incarceration in the United States "mass" incarceration because it is more precisely the "hyperincarceration" of a specific group of people: low-income African American men living in the inner cities. The "cumulative risk of imprisonment for African American males without a high-school diploma tripled between 1979 and 1999, to reach the astonishing rate of 59 percent."[12] "On any given day," notes Roberts, "nearly one-third of black men in their twenties are under the supervision of the criminal justice system—either behind bars, on probation, or on parole."[13]

The system's failings have been widely acknowledged at every level of government. While in office, former attorney general Holder, at the time the nation's highest ranking and most visible criminal justice professional, proclaimed that his colleagues need to be "smarter on crime," meaning more sensible about sentencing for nonviolent or low level offenses and more conscious of the racial biases of current practice.[14] Though Holder applauded the professionalism of his colleagues standing at the gateway to prison—the attorneys, prosecutors, and judges—"smarter on crime" means that status quo tough sentences and racial bias do not lead to safer streets; they are "dumb." Holder's remarks were just the most prominent instance of professional self-criticism pointing to how criminal justice institutions are out of alignment with the people they were meant to serve: the victims and communities affected by offenses, but also the offenders themselves, who are also citizens and both deserve fair and appropriate treatment inside prison and require some constructive way of transitioning to law-abiding life.

Democracy Outside: Increased Activism following Police Shootings

If on the inside of criminal justice institutions we see professionals at all levels doubting the purpose, efficacy, and fairness of their work, on the outside we have witnessed, in the last three years, some of the most dramatic citizen protests in a generation confirming these doubts and pressing for changes— in policing, specifically, but also to address racial inequality in sentencing, the overuse of incarceration, inhumane prison conditions, and the degraded civic status of ex-offenders. DeRay Mckesson, a prominent activist in what became known as Black Lives Matter, left his school administration job in Minneapolis one week after the Michael Brown killing in Ferguson, Missouri, on August 9, 2014. Traveling first to St. Louis, then to New York, to Milwaukee, to North Charleston, and Baltimore, Mckesson has protested, documented other activists as they have marched, held candlelight vigils, blocked traffic, and broadcasted news and images of the events via social media. With little rest in-between, Mckesson moved from city to city following the most recent episode of police violence: "Justice is not an abstract concept" he tweeted during this period, "Justice is a living Mike Brown. Justice is Tamir playing outside again. Justice is Darren Wilson in jail."[15]

The Ferguson protests cast a glaring light on what many in African American communities had understood for decades: the police often operate as a brutal occupying force that approach citizens in these neighborhoods as potential threats rather than human beings. Activists drew national attention to the sharp, painful connections between the many episodes of police killing as pressure grew for change:

> The specter of crisis was also bolstered by cops' simple inability to stop killing Black people. Just prior to Brown's murder, forty-six-year-old Eric Garner of Staten Island, New York, unarmed and minding his own business, was approached by police and then choked to death as he gasped eleven times, "I can't breathe." Two days after Brown was killed, Los Angeles Police Department (LAPD) officers shot and killed another young Black man, Ezell Ford. . . . In a suburb of Dayton, Ohio, police shot to death John Crawford III, twenty-two years old and African American, while he was talking on his

cell phone and holding an air gun on sale in the aisle of a Walmart. And as the nation waited to hear whether a grand jury would indict officer Darren Wilson for Brown's death, Cleveland police killed thirty-seven-year-old, African American Tanisha Anderson when they slammed her to the ground, remaining on top of her until her body went limp. The following week, police in Cleveland struck again, murdering a twelve-year-old boy, Tamir Rice, less than two seconds after arriving at the playground where Rice was playing alone.[16]

Protestors demanded greater transparency in police-involved homicides, the demilitarization of police departments, swift disciplinary measures for officers who have used force, and the abolition of racial profiling practices.

Street activism, large-scale social networking, and citizen journalism have made some significant headway. They have prompted increased mainstream media awareness, Department of Justice investigations into race and policing, speedier reaction to police misconduct among many departments, and commitments to reform from mayors and police chiefs. In North Charleston, South Carolina, for example, the police officer who shot Walter Scott as he was running away was arrested on murder charges the same day as the shooting. In Baltimore, following the death of Freddie Gray in police custody, the mayor called for an independent federal investigation of policing, which resulted in a consent decree outlining clear reforms.[17] Concrete changes to police practice have also resulted. Major departments across the country have increased their use of body cameras and pledged greater transparency to police-involved shootings. The insiders have felt great pressure for reform from the outsiders.

The initial activism of Black Lives Matter was followed by reaction of opponents stressing, once again, a "tough on crime" theme along with a chorus of "Blue Lives Matter," and, among supporters, a period of strategizing about how to achieve greater transformation within the criminal justice system. How to "go from direct action, die-ins, highway closures, and walkouts to ending police brutality without dedicated spaces to meet, strategize, and engage in democratic decision-making?"[18] Reformers inside and activists outside have started to grapple with how deeply resistant criminal justice institutions are and how repellent they can be to citizen agency and thus to lasting changes. "Protests can do many things, but protests alone cannot end police abuse and the conditions that are used to justify it," writes Taylor.[19] Routine, not extraordinary, linkages must be forged between active and alert communities, and reform-minded professionals within criminal justice institutions, as well

as constructively engaging with those who react to demands for change by
defending "law and order."

Restorative Justice Reform

External and internal pressures to rethink and reform criminal justice professionalism are helping strengthen the view that social order is everyone's business, and that to be done well and fairly, a greater sense of public ownership
must emerge to check the coercive apparatuses of the state, but also to notice and address the harmful situations and conflicts that get translated into
crimes. One way this democratic sensibility is already being encouraged—
in part by opening up criminal justice practices to greater citizen awareness
and participation—is through restorative justice. Since the 1970s, restorative
justice programs across the country have involved offenders in structured
dialogues with victims, victim surrogates, and sometimes with other members
of an affected community. The process is typically facilitated by a volunteer
mediator who is not a court professional or official.[20] Juvenile, misdemeanor,
and other low-level offenders freely choose the restorative justice track, if one
is available to them. After reflective dialogues with affected parties or their
proxies, a successful restorative justice case ends in restitution, apology, or
some other form of recompense rather than a penalty. If an offender fails
to meet the demands of the restorative justice process, then his or her case
defaults back to the formal criminal justice system.

Present in every state in the United States, though most widely used in
a handful of states including California, Pennsylvania, Minnesota, Texas,
Colorado, Arizona, New York, Ohio, and Alaska, restorative justice has become one of the most extensive and deeply embedded criminal justice reform
efforts in the last quarter century.[21] In part this is because of its ideological
expansiveness and institutional flexibility. Ideologically, it brings together
faith-based and social justice advocates of a more peaceful resolution to social problems, libertarians eager to shrink state involvement, and victims'
rights advocates pushing for greater voice and appreciation for victims; it has
appealed to seasoned veterans within the halls of criminal justice administration as well as doggedly idealistic community activists. Restorative justice
programs are housed in mayors' offices, lower courts, prosecutors' offices, and
departments of corrections, and in nongovernmental community organizations as well.[22]

Many practitioners and advocates of restorative justice do not talk about
their work in democratic terms, however, tending to favor communitarian

over participatory democratic rhetoric. At one level, this is unsurprising, as too much democracy via populist referenda and "tough on crime" electoral posturing is commonly blamed for the sentencing severity of measures such as three-strikes legislation and for over-incarceration more generally.[23] Also, just like those school principals in the previous chapter who prefer to frame discussion of participatory practices in terms of "student voice" or "active learning community" rather than "democracy" for fear of sparking ideological controversy, criminal justice reformers operate in a tense, politically charged environment. Yet the three major thinkers in restorative justice, Nils Christie, Howard Zehr, and John Braithwaite, clearly understand its practices to be about increasing citizen control over institutions that are currently out of alignment with victims, offenders, and the communities they purportedly serve.[24] Restorative justice programs vary in the kinds of citizen participation they foster, but most rely in some way on the integration of lay volunteers into the professionalized domain of adjudication.

Democratic Practices in Criminal Justice

Of the three professionalized fields examined by this project, criminal justice institutions are the most prima facie undemocratic. They involve coercive power that is wielded asymmetrically, they impose rigid and stigmatizing hierarchies, and they are marked by inequalities throughout. For these reasons as well as because of their repellent nature—understood in the terms discussed in Chapter 2—they are rarely topics of discussion in democratic theory.[25] Yet much is happening under the surface. While dominant tendencies incline toward managerial control, professionalized divisions of labor, and bureaucratic rigidity, there are instructive examples of democratic agency emerging precisely in some of the worst-off places. We consider here four sites of innovation: nongovernmental community organizations, police departments, schools, and prisons. Drawing from background research and interviews with reformers, we will note motivations for encouraging citizen participation, discuss barriers to change, and identify resources available to sustain and expand innovation. While still sparse on the ground, these innovative practices help challenge prevailing assumptions that criminal justice institutions are inherently undemocratic and must involve coercion, hierarchy, and inequality.

It should be noted that the democratic ideal is far from foreign to American criminal justice institutions, as the participatory democratic institution of the jury enjoys constitutional entrenchment and deep public

support. Indeed, the jury can offer a robust example of democratic professionalism in action—when it works well—for through it court professionals
share adjudicatory power in a horizontal fashion with lay citizens who are
understood to have something valuable to contribute to matters of grave
personal and civic importance. Yet over the course of the twentieth century the power being shared declined to the point where juries are tiny
cogs in a bureaucratic criminal justice process.[26] Not only do they handle
only a small fraction of the total criminal indictments, as we have noted,
they are highly constrained in the way they do so. Confronting the margin-
alization of jurors and juries, democracy-minded reformers have advocated
increasing the number of trials by interrupting the plea-bargaining process and reducing the costs of juries, empowering jurors to ask questions
during the trial and not merely during deliberations, and granting juries
a degree of sentencing authority after reaching a verdict. Such reforms are
distant from everyday practice in most jurisdictions, but a growing number
of sympathetic court professionals embrace them, knowing that serious repairs are needed if the jury system is to survive.[27]

To revive the jury in a remodeled and renovated form, however, a broad
respect for citizen agency and capacity among professionals and lay citizens
alike must be more firmly embraced. This is where democratic professional
efforts play a constructive role throughout the formal and quasi-formal sites
of criminal justice. Participatory innovations in police departments, schools,
prisons, and community organizations can bring people—who may rather be
doing something else—into the work of criminal justice. These are efforts in
power-sharing, but they also have to do with learning to care about what is
happening to people around you, and taking some responsibility, some share
of public ownership, for social ordering and repair.

Community Justice

While most restorative justice programs have significant roles for lay volunteers
and seek greater community involvement and voice in adjudication, some
show greater commitment to widespread participation and substantive task-
sharing. Community Reparative Boards in Vermont, for example, are staffed
by citizen volunteers and hold their meetings in public places such as libraries,
community centers, town halls, and police stations.[28] They conduct dialogues
with offenders convicted but not sentenced for nonviolent offenses such as
underage drinking, impaired driving, and shoplifting. They seek to communicate the meaning of the harm for the victims involved, to determine how to

repair whatever damage was done, and to consider how to avoid such action in the future. The outcome of dialogues is a contract with offenders involving community service, reparation, apology and the like.[29] Other explicitly participatory programs, such as those of the Community Conferencing Center of Baltimore, Maryland, respond to referrals from police, prosecutors, schools, and community organizations by conducting neighborhood dialogues concerning conflicts that have not yet become formal offenses.[30]

Lauren Abramson is the founder of Baltimore's Community Conferencing Center, an organization that aims to divert people from the criminal justice system before they enter it by providing "a highly participatory community-based process for people to transform their conflicts into cooperation, take collective and personal responsibility for action, and improve their quality of life."[31] Abramson's center has helped thousands of people address problems in their communities before they become formally designated as crimes to be handled by the justice system.

To illustrate, consider a story I call "Football Trouble." Not long ago, Abramson's center was called on to handle a typical neighborhood problem. All was not well on Streeper Street in Southeast Baltimore. Kids played football in the road late into the night, bumping into cars, setting off alarms, breaking mirrors and windows. Why couldn't they play in the park just two blocks away? Were they selling drugs in the street rather than just playing football? Tensions between adult residents and the players escalated into arguments, hundreds of calls to the police, and petty retaliations such as putting sugar in gas tanks. Finally, when police interventions didn't succeed and the conflict threatened to get more serious than minor property damage, a neighborhood organization contacted the Community Conferencing Center to arrange a meeting with those affected.

One of the Center's facilitators, Misty, canvassed the neighborhood for three weeks, going door-to-door inviting everyone to participate in a conference where they could articulate concerns and contribute to a desirable and workable solution. Remaining neutral, she encouraged attendance by showing them a list of those who had already agreed to participate. In all, forty-four people attended, with a mix of adults and youth.

The conference began with angry comments. Parents defended their children against what they felt was unfair treatment by neighbors. In turn, the adult residents expressed their frustration over the late night noise created by the football games: Was this really the best place to play football at night? The children explained that the park two blocks away that the adults thought was much safer than the street was actually fouled by dog waste at one end and inhabited by drug dealers and older bullies at the other—problems that the adults had not heard before. From that point on, the neighbors started brainstorming possible solutions. They shifted focus from what to do about a bunch of noisy young people to how to find a safe place for the neighborhood children to play. Misty asked how they might put their solutions into practice, and in less than half an hour the group had come to an agreement on a list of actions, such as adults volunteering to chaperone in the park and youth helping clean up the neighborhood.

The next day, in fact, community member Don Ferges chaperoned twenty-two kids in the park. By the end of three weeks, the number had grown to sixty-four, and by the end of the summer there was a thriving football league. What started out as a public nuisance warranting police action developed into neighborhood-wide recognition of common interests and action to improve the space they shared. The residents had the power to make these changes, but it took a well-structured and facilitated conference to deliberate and act together.

Reflecting on this blend of community-self-development and outside facilitation, Abramson explains, "We've defined 'community' as the community of people who have been affected by and involved in the conflict or the crime. Everybody who's involved in or affected by the situation, and their respective supporters, is included." Community conferences can be as big as needed to address a particular problem. "We really widen the circle," Abramson says. "Thus, conferences usually include between ten and forty people. The Streeper Street neighborhood conflict had been going on for two years and forty-four people attended. Conferences are always about engaging the entire community of people affected by whatever's going on and giving them the power to try to fix it."[32]

Organizers of community conferences use a deceptively simple process. First, they gather together in one place everyone affected by a harmful action. Then, they encourage each person, one at a time, to tell the group what happened. Then, again, another round of contributions as each participant tells the group how it affects them personally and how they feel about it. Finally, participants say what they want to do about the action to move forward. It is a simple process, but crucial normative choices are built into it. Especially important is the freedom to be passionate, sad, and even angry. Few limits are placed on emotions in a community conference because organizers believe that public expression of emotions brings them out in a safe space where they can be observed, felt, and become part of a collective practice. Relatedly, few limits are placed on speech:

Conferencing is elegant. There are three questions that the group's going to talk about. And they can talk in whatever way they want. We don't go in saying, "You can't make racist comments," because if you do that then the person who is racist is never going to get a chance to change. We let the group decide. So once something offensive comes up, the facilitator will say to the participants: "There is a request to not say these kinds of things, is this something everyone can agree to?" It lets people be who they are and then lets that group decide for itself the norms for their behavior from this time forward.[33]

Difficult, even mean-spirited, words are acceptable in a conference because it is better to have them out in public—and potentially subject to contestation—than withheld and simmering inside individuals.

Abramson insists that the conferencing process does not repair social problems for people, but rather serves as a medium for them to handle their own problems in their own way. "We need to look at what *structures* we offer people in our society to resolve conflict and crime, because they determine the outcomes. The fact that people in highly distressed neighborhoods can negotiate solutions within the structure provided by Community Conferencing only emphasizes the fact that we are all capable of safely and effectively resolving many of our own conflicts." Participatory innovations such as conferencing, notes Abramson, recognize and affirm, "that we all have a larger capacity to resolve complicated conflicts and crimes than we are allowed to. But people also need to have an appropriate structure to do it." It is a process that challenges conventional public and official attitudes grown comfortable with the typically hierarchical decision-making in criminal justice. As Abramson argues, "if our institutions are top-down—if we need a judge in a black robe telling people how they should be punished—then we're going to get one set of outcomes. But if we engage people with this alternative structure—in a circle where they acknowledge what happened, share how they've been affected, and then decide how to make it better—then we will get a whole different set of outcomes."[34]

While restorative justice practitioners such as Abramson are openly critical of mainstream criminal justice, they are also realists. They realize that to be successful, reforms must be done in connection to established institutions rather than against them:

Restorative justice programs bring about reform from both the bottom up and the top down. In Baltimore, our juvenile courts are diverting

felony and misdemeanor cases from their system to Community
Conferencing. Could they refer more cases than they do? Absolutely.
But for them to take a felony case and say, "We think these people
can resolve it better through Community Conferencing than through
our system," that's a significant change. And every year around 1,400
people in Baltimore participate in a Community Conference.

Has it completely changed our criminal justice system? No.
But when judges call us and ask us how they can use Community
Conferencing more, I know that we are making progress.[35]

Restorative justice conferences thus become circulatory channels between
a professionalized domain and neighborhoods taking up the task of co-
producing social order.

Similarly, reformers view public attitudes toward crime and punishment
both skeptically and realistically; involving citizens rather than managing for
them is crucial to moving toward a less punitive future. Abramson's participatory form of restorative justice is not used *after* a community has come to recognize its responsibilities for deliberate thought and action regarding social
order; it is used *before*, as part of a community-building process. As Abramson
stresses, "the more people you involve in the justice process the more potential there is for community building. Imagine justice that builds a sense of
community. If only two people are involved, the potential for building community is very limited. That's why we use the process we do. I love the fact
that nobody talks on behalf of anybody else. Inclusion has a ripple effect and
we include all the ripples."[36] Kay Pranis, who served as a statewide restorative justice planner for the Minnesota Department of Corrections, agrees that
participatory innovations such as conferences are ways of organizing community reactions to crime while also guiding, focusing, and drawing upon
citizen capabilities for healing and rebuilding: "If there is a robbery in your
neighborhood, there is a whole bunch of energy around that. This is initially
negative energy. The restorative processes—particularly circles because they
can engage more people—give you a way to transform the negative energy
that arises naturally into positive community-building energy."[37]

Highly participatory restorative justice programs such as Abramson's
Community Conferencing are uncommon but not unique. Community
Works, in Oakland, California, and Red Hook Community Justice in
Brooklyn, New York, operate along similar lines. Community Works, for ex-
ample, partners with the San Francisco District Attorney to divert juveniles
who would otherwise go through the normal juvenile criminal court process.

In facilitated conferences, these young people meet with victims and other members of an affected community to come to a better understanding of the harms caused by the acts and to form a plan for addressing the harms. Upon successful completion of the plan, the juveniles are no longer subject to criminal charges.[38] For reform-minded professionals inside courts, police departments, and corrections agencies and nongovernmental actors outside, participatory restorative justice spreads responsibility for criminal justice more broadly.

Community Policing, Citizen Advisory Boards, and Procedural Justice

Policing has been a major recent flashpoint drawing public attention to problems of racism, fairness, and brutality in criminal justice. In 2016 there were nearly a thousand fatal police shootings and scores of protest marches, vigils, and sit-ins across the country.[39] In many cities, this activism has prompted police departments to increase their transparency and reaction times in responding to officer-involved shootings. Yet conventional "tough on crime" rhetoric has also enjoyed surprising resurgence in partisan political discourse at the highest levels. At the Republican National Convention, in an acceptance speech that used the phrase "law and order" four times, the nominee sharply criticized citizen protestors: "I have a message to every last person threatening the peace on our streets and the safety of our police: When I take the oath of office next year, I will restore law and order to our country."[40] Crime surfaced again in the most dramatic phrase of the new president's inaugural address: "the crime and the gangs and the drugs that have stolen too many lives and robbed our country of so much unrealized potential. This American carnage stops right here and stops right now."[41]

Less noticed than these proactive and reactive calls to action, but potentially significant for long-term reform of repellent criminal justice institutions, are efforts at opening police departments to more community participation. Closely related to restorative justice programs, but typically offering citizens fewer load-bearing roles, are the numerous community policing programs across the country. These involve advisory bodies composed of citizens who meet regularly with key criminal justice actors in an evaluative as well as problem-solving capacity. As David Sklansky notes, community policing emerged in the 1980s and consolidated in the 1990s into a prominent repudiation of one form of orthodox police professionalism that had become "arrogant, heavy-handed, technologically driven, and aloof." "The notion that the police should work with communities, rather than against them, became the heart of the community policing movement."[42]

The "community beat meetings" held by the Chicago Police Department since 1993, for example, create channels of communication between officers—who make the all important street-level decisions that open the gates of the criminal justice process—and members of distressed neighborhoods impacted by both crime and incarceration. Facilitated by civilians, these regularly scheduled hour-long meetings bring residents together monthly with the police officers who patrol their neighborhoods. There, citizens can articulate their concerns about gangs, violence, theft, social disorder, dilapidated and abandoned buildings, traffic, parking, and even the competence and conduct of the police. Citizens also learn about the progress or lack of progress on previously raised issues and brainstorm ways of solving them. As Wesley Skogan writes about the Chicago experience, citizens involved in beat meetings are "setting the agenda for police and community action, monitoring the effectiveness of police responses to community priorities, and mobilizing residents to act on their own behalf."[43]

Citizen advisory bodies are present in other institutional locations, too, such as the community prosecution efforts in Portland, Denver, Indianapolis, and elsewhere. In Denver, for example, prosecutors have formed "community justice councils that provide direct community input into the definition and prioritization of problems, and the development and implementation of remedies to solve those problems."[44] Citizen advisory bodies such as these have been characterized as democratic innovations by reform-minded scholars, though activists may favor social justice terms to describe them and professional practitioners may view them as instruments of achieving transparency and fairness, avenues for improving community relations, and ways of regaining trust and legitimacy.[45]

Related police reforms are occurring under the name of "procedural justice" to directly address the perceptions of unfairness that drive citizen distrust of police, especially among African Americans. In many neighborhoods the police are experienced as a kind of occupying force that lacks respect for community members—routinely treating them in ways they would never consider if faced with their own family members or neighbors. Procedural justice reformers urge police to follow clear and fair rules that leave citizens with the understanding that justice is being done transparently, consistently, and fairly. They advocate rethinking what it means to be professional. Police officers, notes procedural justice advocate Tom Tyler, need to "move from a harm reduction model to a community engagement approach" to police professionalism. This means shifting from "warrior" to "guardian" attitudes, as well as treating people as more than clients or threats but as citizens with something to contribute to "comanaging social order," and it means finding ways to contribute, themselves, to social capital production in neighborhoods.[46]

Procedural justice and community policing efforts might best be characterized as proto-democratic innovations, as it is not clear yet how deep police departments' commitment to power-sharing with lay citizens is in most cases. Though practitioners have "appealed in part to the sense that community policing is 'more democratic than conventional policing,' because it improves 'the public's capacity to influence policing,'" Sklansky points out that both the policing roles played by community members and the community-related actions of the police are often more symbolic than substantive:

> The rhetoric of community policing . . . calls for the police to be partners of the community, not part of the community itself. In reality, the relationship falls far short of true partnership: community policing as actually practiced rarely intrudes much on the operational autonomy of the police. But community policing does even less to make the police a genuine part of the community. Almost always, a police department engaged in community policing remains, in every significant respect, "a force of outsiders."[47]

As Clifford Shearing argues, community policing typically leaves the tasks of social order firmly in the professional domain of police departments, with the citizens helping the police with "their" job rather than co-producing justice alongside police.[48] Similarly, absent a strong commitment to lay power-sharing, the democratic possibilities of procedural justice are easily dampened.

Participatory Conflict Resolution in Schools

Another site of participatory innovation in criminal justice is found in schools. Nearly a century ago Dewey argued against traditional textbook civics education that merely lectured students on law. A proper civic education, Dewey insisted, would provide students a truly collaborative environment at school; education for democracy requires acting democratically. To understand the meaning of core ideals of procedural fairness or political equality, for example, "involves a context of work and play in association with others." "Social perceptions and interests," he wrote, "can be developed only in a genuinely social medium—one where there is give and take in the building up of a common experience."[49] The contemporary educational reformers we encountered in the last chapter who give children a steering role in shaping curricula, advising new teachers, and solving institutional problems are following in Dewey's path. The education in criminal justice I want to focus on here means allowing young people to make decisions early and often on how to cope with norm-breaking. Such experiential learning fosters the self-realization of being "centinels and guardians of each other"—to borrow, again, the eighteenth century phrase used to honor jury duty.

Early experience with collective decision-making regarding social norms and group expectations may be effective in activating and encouraging capabilities even while not closely resembling either the form or the substance of typical adult adjudication. Vivian Gussin Paley, an intellectual descendent of Dewey's who also worked in Chicago's Lab Schools, noticed a recurrent problem in her primary school classroom. The most popular students had a surplus of playmates at recess while others, much to their shame and disappointment, were constantly excluded. After meetings with the children, and referring to this painful, if invisible, issue through an ongoing series of animal stories, Paley and the youth formulated a simple rule: "You Can't Say You Can't Play." Marginalized children could present this rule to those in more popular groups in order to gain admission to games they would normally have to witness from the sidelines. With the rule in hand they could stand up for themselves and have recourse, as well, with their teachers and playground monitors. By taking part in rule-making and rule-enforcement, these children learned—by doing—important lessons in self-governance and participatory social control.[50]

Another example comes from the Bathroom Busters, a group of St. Paul middle schoolers troubled by restrooms covered in graffiti, lacking in privacy because of broken stalls, and chronically short of soap and paper. Through the innovative Public Achievement program, they learned how to work with an inefficient school bureaucracy and to communicate with parents, teachers, and administrators to gain the resources needed to repaint walls, repair missing stall doors, and replenish needed supplies.[51] A problem that might have been seen as a juvenile offense, to be handled by school administrators and police officers, was translated into a social problem taken up by the students who refused to have institutions think and act for them.

Finally, consider a story I call "Basketball Blowup," which takes place in one of the schools we encountered in the last chapter, Forest Grove Community School, in Oregon.[52] During recess one spring day, some 7th-grade students were playing basketball. Classroom tensions spilled over into the game. Two boys closely guarding another boy stole the ball from him, repeatedly. He got mad and lashed out, hitting one of the opponents.

When the victim's father was notified that his son was hit, he immediately asked the principal to suspend the offender, or else the father would call the police and charge the boy with assault. Principal Vanessa Gray had a different idea. After reassuring the parent, she began by meeting with a group of students who were on the playground at the time of the incident to talk about what happened. Then she brought all three of the basketball players into her office one by one. The bystanders and the main actors all confirmed that the facts of the case were not in dispute. Principal Gray allowed the victim to go home, sent his teammate back to class, and kept the perpetrator in her office for a while to talk.

Over the course of their conversation, she came to understand that the perpetrator needed to develop his communication skills for times when he feels stressed and frustrated. She explained, "You always have a voice. You don't have to hit somebody to make a point. Your voice can get loud; sometimes that's appropriate to say, 'Back OFF!!' really loudly. That gets the point across." Telling him she understood his frustration, she also made it clear that it is not acceptable to communicate with his fists.

In addition, Principal Gray took responsibility for her own role in the conflict, acknowledging to the perpetrator that he had come to her earlier in the year to say that basketball games could get overly aggressive. "This is really helpful for me to do a better job of trying to understand what a kid is communicating to me," Gray said, "and for you, kid, to learn a little more about how to use your voice. The way you expressed the tensions on the basketball court earlier this school year was in the same tone you use when you tell me that school is boring or you are going skiing this weekend. What you said did not make me concerned that you were angry. And I'm wondering if your way of expressing your frustration with your classmates has also been similarly flat and that you need to work on feeling more comfortable with saying 'Hey I'm upset!' 'I'm mad!' 'I want someone to do something about it!' 'I want someone to work with me on this.'" Before sending him home for the day, she told him that there were going to be further conversations when he came back to school.

The next day the conferencing began, and Principal Gray told the three students they cannot play basketball until they have a congress with all the basketball players about what the rules are going to be as they go forward with the game. She later relates, "I really wanted these three to understand: they messed up the basketball game. And I wanted the other basketball players to understand that they were bystanders. They knew that these tensions were going on a long time before it erupted and before I knew about it. I wanted them to understand they had a responsibility to right a wrong and there are lots of ways for them to do it."

Rather than sealing off a problem, attributing blame to a specific central actor, and taking ownership of it as simple disciplinary matter for the administration to take care of, Principal Gray did four things: she made the problem public; she had conversations with everyone involved; she spread out responsibility for the conflict, herself included; and she empowered everyone involved—including bystanders and others in the school—to figure out ways of creating more peaceful basketball games at recess. Yes, there was an offense that happened that should not have, and yes, there was an offender and a victim. But the participatory process Gray used focused on the relationships that were causing tension, and that focus allowed her to help students themselves play a bigger role in solving the problem by working on the skills they need to have better relationships in the future.

Just like the citizens involved with Lauren Abramson's community justice center, Forest Grove Community School students are learning—by doing—important lessons in how to work and live together. Gray is introducing people as far as they are capable into an institutional field of self-government. Her school is fostering a more deliberative and more collaborative mode of being together through everyday routines performed by students, teachers, and administrators who refuse to let themselves be captured by conventional assumptions about the dependency of disciplinary order on institutional hierarchies. Civic engagement is not a freestanding class or a subject area in this school, nor is it an extracurricular activity; it pervades the culture of the playground, the library, the hallways, the assembly rooms, the school garden, and the principal's office.

While the last example is drawn from an explicitly democratic school, the other two were not. Indeed, there is considerable interest in participatory innovation in conflict resolution across the United States in otherwise nondemocratic schools. School districts have come to understand the negative consequences of tough-minded "zero tolerance" policies meting out expulsion and other exclusionary penalties for disciplinary problems: increased disengagement from school for penalized youth, who are shunted from school to school and are more likely to eventually enter the formal criminal justice system via the so-called "school to prison" pipeline. Public schools in cities such as Baltimore, Boston, Chicago, Cleveland, Denver, Minneapolis, and New York have thus felt a pressing need to experiment with more restorative and participatory programs.

Prisons as Sites of Participatory Reflection and Public Awareness

Severe limits are placed on lay citizen involvement in prisons, but there are also many ways for innovative professionals to open up these restrictive environments from the inside and demand access points from the outside. Prison education programs such as Inside-Out, which link college and university teachers and students with groups of current prisoners, do more than provide educational opportunities for inmates. They also embody a form of professional power-sharing regarding the task of rehabilitation and penitential reflection, they dissolve distances between citizens and inmates, and they create spaces for public dialogue inside and outside about prison life and the reality of punishment. Over 600 Inside-Out courses exist across the United States, in more than one hundred correctional facilities. More than 22,000 people have taken these credit-bearing courses, which bring fifteen to eighteen college students together with the same number of inmates for a few hours every week for one semester.[53] They participate as fellow members of the same class, usually focused on issues of criminal justice, and work together on a class project.[54] Other arrangements between universities and prisons have emerged organically, using the Inside-Out model as a starting point.

Lisa Guenther, a philosopher at Vanderbilt University, has held reading groups in a maximum security prison in Nashville with six graduate student "outsiders" and six "insiders" who are inmates, including some on death row. The small size of the group and its meeting schedule were established through negotiation with the prison administration, while the type of student who could join was the subject of negotiation with the university administration, which permitted graduate but not undergraduate students. Guenther's group engages in wide-ranging discussions driven largely by prisoners' interests. Recently, they read Plato's dialogues concerning the trial and punishment of Socrates, which became a way of talking about the prison experience that otherwise would have been difficult:

> [W]e weren't talking about prison in some kind of stark direct way. That can turn into a kind of voyeuristic situation where the insiders are expected to be experts on suffering in prison and the outsiders, who know little or nothing about prison, go to them to be educated. Weird

power dynamics can unfold in a situation where you bring together people who often have very different economic, racial, gender social positions and also different levels of formal education. Everything we do is about negotiating that terrain and trying to create and recreate the space for meaningful conversation through and across these chasms of social inequality. You cannot undo inequality by just having the best intentions to treat everyone as a singular human being. You really have to work at creating the situation in which a conversation can happen and keep happening. Plato helped in ways I had not anticipated to open up a situation where we have a third term in the room. We all had the character of Socrates to look at and to talk about and we could bring different insights or different perspectives to bear on that third term.[55]

Connections made between the reading group and the prison catalyzed further outside work, such as an art show held on campus exhibiting work done by the inmates in the group, and campus workshops and conferences related to mass incarceration, as well as community organizing on the death penalty. Prisoners have helped "develop a kind of activist practice within the group focused on issues that have been identified by the insiders as of central importance to them." These are not always what outsiders would expect. "One of the extraordinary things to me," notes Guenther, "is that abolishing the death penalty was definitely not first on their list. The issues that everyone agrees are the most important are medical care—or lack thereof—and the school-to-prison pipeline, so broad-based social transformations such that kids would not be funneled into the prison system, and not end up in a place like they are."[56] It is a slow, long-term strategy, she indicates, aiming not at electoral politics but "the level of the demos understood as people, socially situated, with broad, intersectional concerns."

Closing distances between citizens and inmates and reflecting, together, on crime and punishment and justice, opening spaces for dialogue inside and outside prisons; these efforts can appear abstract, timid, overly academic in the face of mass incarceration. Yet they are actually hard-nosed practical efforts. Not only do these interventions strike at a root cause of the problem, namely the social distance between the public and our institutions of punishment, but they do so without raising the red flag of political activism that would trigger administrative denial of security privileges for lay citizen efforts inside, such as reading groups. By moving, if only incrementally, some of the most repellent American institutions into the routines of "normal" society, these reformers are taking up significant work.

Some prison education programs result in full-fledged college degrees. An early proponent is the Bard Prison Initiative (BPI), which offers liberal arts education across six New York state prisons. Incarcerated women and men who gain admission to the highly selective program take courses equivalent to those offered on the main Bard campus and earn the same degrees. BPI offers over sixty courses per semester and has grown from an initial fifteen-student cohort to an enrollment of over three hundred incarcerated men and women. To date Bard has granted over 350 degrees to BPI participants.

The overarching purpose of the program is to share the criminal justice professional task of rehabilitation and reintegration by providing inmates with the educational resources needed to find a place in society. As BPI founder Max Kenner notes:

> BPI . . . creates opportunities for people later in life to work hard to achieve real fulfillment, to get sense of the breadth of one's own curiosity, to engage with the world in an entirely different way. And, it happens that we do this with the people who the last generation of America's best social scientists called "super predators" and "hopeless." Most concretely, the vast majority of our students go into the human services or they do advocacy after they are released from prison. They are working with people who are homeless, with youth at risk, people returning home from prison, people with HIV and AIDS, etc. They do God's work, they do work that desperately needs to be done well, and they are highly qualified for it. The vast majority of our people are returning to the communities that send the most people to prison. And they do so with two qualities employers in those fields always want but virtually never come together: people who have really "been there" and have had first hand experience and are "authentic," on the one hand, but who also have a really rigorous and unusual education.

A college degree program has a ripple effect on a prison, balancing its carceral elements with a wider range of transformative possibilities. The "signal the program is sending to the entire prison population," says Kenner, is that "there is a path. It may be hard to get to but you know there is a path to something different. And you know that is true for your children. And you know that is true for how your children perceive you."

The human capacity a program such as BPI can release is strikingly illustrated by a story Kenner relates, which we can call "What about Latvia?"[57]

A few weeks ago the debate team from the University of Vermont walks into the auditorium at Eastern Correctional Facility in upstate New York. Three of them, preppy, young. Our guys are all in their 30s. Rodney came to prison as a 20-year-old doing 20 to life. Paul is not an obvious candidate for debate; he rarely speaks, but he is thriving in calculus. And Daryl is getting set to complete his degree. However electric the room, they all seem remarkably calm.

I am not.

Resolve: NATO should be immediately abolished. Our guys are arguing the negatives. They have not had access to the Internet for research or e-mail for professional advice, no debate camps. UVM's team is ranked 14th in the world. After 45 minutes of arguing, it is over. UVM, one of the top programs on the planet. Our guys did their best.

And after some discussion, the judges reach a decision. The incarcerated Bard students had won.

Afterwards everyone shakes hands. When our students are alone they take stock. In the end the UVM team missed their golden opportunity. "What about Latvia?" Rodney says. "I mean how could they not mention Latvia."

I have no idea what he is talking about. But there is no time for him to explain. The guards return to take them back to their other lives and their 8-by-11 cells.

While BPI offers learning opportunities for inmates, it is also indirectly challenging the perceptions of inmates among those working—and competing—with them from the outside.

There is surprisingly broad academic support for BPI at the college, evidenced by the waiting list of faculty eager to teach seminars in prisons and the considerable pride in the program displayed by the traditional undergraduate population. Some of the loudest moments in campus commencement ceremonies are when BPI students receive their degree. For faculty and students alike, the program illustrates the value of a liberal arts degree to shape lives and to transform society. While not conventionally "political," this kind of effort lowers barriers between elite and disadvantaged, citizen and noncitizen. As Kenner reflects, "one can imagine us as a kind of Highlander school in the era of mass incarceration. We are not training people just to be civic advocates in one way or another, of course. Not by any stretch. We are thrilled when alumni go into business, or when they go into the arts, or the ministry or what have you. But there is a sort of physics to the work: if you ensure that the places in society that are worst off have outlets for people to become the best they can be, unexpected and profound things can happen."

Bard is a leader in these efforts, but it is not the only liberal arts school extending a full range of teaching into prisons. The recently created Consortium for the Liberal Arts in Prison joins together Bennington, Emerson, Grinnell, Goucher, Holy Cross, Yale, Notre Dame, the University of Vermont, Washington University, and Wesleyan in establishing high-level teaching programs for inmates.

William DiMascio, as head of the Pennsylvania Prison Society, has experimented with a different kind of participatory innovation. DiMascio has organized deliberative forums involving visitors and inmates in every prison in the state. These forums involve moderated small-group dialogue about current issues such as social security, healthcare policy, and school violence, which are laid out in nonpartisan booklets published by the National Issues Forums Institute. "Our intention was manifold," notes DiMascio, "first, we wanted to get forums going in the prison; second, we wanted . . . reluctant prison administrators to see the interest and value in permitting the forums to take place; and third, to stimulate interest in public deliberation."[58]

As with Guenther's graduate seminar and Kenner's high-level curriculum behind bars, one purpose of DiMascio's deliberative forum is empowerment. Here, within the space of a moderated group discussion, a person has the freedom to form his or her own opinion on something, to express it to others, and to shape an ongoing group discussion. After a first round of forums, which DiMascio spearheaded, inmates in a number of prisons requested further sessions.

> There is a thirst, if you will, to be heard, to be relevant, to feel like people can engage with them, people are interested in hearing what their opinions are. And this is something they are deprived of, for the most part, while they are in prison. You know the steel bars and the big fences and all really cannot prevent that quite natural human desire. So I think that is why they requested them. My goal is to begin to bring marginalized men and women back into a society where their thoughts and feelings are heard.[59]

Prison life is "day in and day out, a pretty dismal and boring existence—one that really reinforces the lack of humanity in everybody who is there," notes DiMascio. "I have always been taken by the fact that in visiting with different

inmates I met some positively brilliant minds. And yet they live in this intellectual wasteland."

While only contingently achieved because of prison administration reluc-
tance, DiMascio's deliberative forums show a concrete process for lay citizens
to interact within local prisons to share experiences and engage in dialogue
with inmates. Such circulation of people and ideas can be seen as a way of
encouraging responsibility for what one thinks and does—whether one is an
inmate or an outsider. By becoming involved, lay citizens can learn indirectly
about the causes and consequences of crime and punishment and achieve a
kind of sobriety about incarceration. "I believe that people would see what
they do not seem to want to see if they would begin to accept responsibility
for what our criminal justice system is doing. The failed system has cost un-
told millions of dollars. I do not think people realize generally that the system
operates the way it does."[60]

Participatory innovation in prison has both the long-term goal of public
awareness and the concrete, short-term objective of improving well-being one
participant at a time. Inmates coming to make choices about what to read,
how to focus their thinking, and how to argue are active citizens in the republic of ideas even as their civic agency is otherwise severely hampered. This
is a democratic education in one of the least democratic places imaginable.[61]

Sustainability and Growth

How can reform-minded criminal justice professionals and their allies
working alongside in schools and community organizations sustain reflective
and participatory practices at a time of significant agitation over criminal justice? While overlapping concerns about racism, inhumanity, and economic
inefficiency link otherwise adversarial political coalitions, these have been
loosened by the revival of atavistic "tough on crime" rhetoric in elections.[62]
In this context, there is newfound relevance for innovations that work in the
background and interstices of institutions and in the surrounding community
environment.

Work in a community justice conference, on a community policing
advisory board, or in a seminar at a prison, or in a conflict resolution
program for a 5th grade classroom may seem trivial given that the bulk
of decision-making in criminal justice institutions proceeds in relatively
non-participatory fashion, but it can make a difference. Restorative justice volunteers, beat meeting participants, and school children repairing
breaches in social order on their own have real existence in political space

and time. They are load-bearing members of the manifold institutions of criminal justice: the particular institutions they are working with are thinking and then acting through them. This kind of thoughtful and responsible action begins as early as elementary school, is called for periodically even if we have not chosen to participate, brings us into close contact with people who differ from us, refuses to segregate those judged from those judging, and contributes to a political culture that becomes better able to see, hear, and talk about difficult subjects.

These innovations are disruptive and constructive. They challenge the idea of criminal justice as a matter to be handled by an authoritative, professionalized body deciding guilt and measuring out punishment. Each in its own way reconstructs criminal justice as a multifaceted process encouraging thinking together about our conflicts, our harmful acts, and what we can do together to repair and prevent them. To do criminal justice in a participatory democracy is to move beyond "locking up the bad guys"; it is to try to do a better job of ordering our social world. Each addresses what Margaret Urban Walker calls our "morally significant non-perception": the ways mainstream practices shield the advantaged from the consequences of policies such as the draconian criminalization of certain drugs that sent Savina Sauceda, whom we met in Chapter 2, to prison.[63] Normal, regular, citizen action inside and outside is required for contemporary publics to soberly acknowledge and assume responsibility for criminal justice institutions.

Three factors seem important to sustainability and growth for participatory innovation in criminal justice. The first is critical mass. Echoing David Mathews' concept of a democratic ecosystem, restorative justice advocates talk about gradual culture change via continual, steady pressure on and in institutions. As Abramson notes:

> [C]ultural change does not happen overnight. Kay Pranis, who is a leader in this country on restorative justice, says restorative justice is like groundwater. Most people don't see groundwater but it nourishes a lot of things. Eventually, it is going to bust through. So has restorative justice fixed everything? No. Is it incrementally making steps toward a tipping point? I would say, most definitely, yes. It is really starting to happen in education. A lot of school systems are talking about restorative practices. But it is going to take a long time to change our cowboy-puritan culture of individuals to begin to look at things as relationships and accountability instead of punishment.

While few think of participatory innovation in criminal justice as part of an overarching social movement, reformers in this area take note of ideas and practices from other domains—sharing hopeful stories and commiserating over setbacks.

Second, and closely related, are the institutional weaknesses that drive professionals on the inside to look to alternative practices and to welcome in new ways of doing traditional tasks. "Tough on crime" may win a few elections, but penal managerialism is extremely costly in human and monetary terms, driving an increasing number of professionals to realize that the bill for getting tough on crime through imprisonment is unaffordable morally and financially even if it can pay short-term political dividends. Throughout criminal justice institutions and alongside them we see professionals willing to take risks on alternative procedures. In the State of Washington, prisons have partnered with university environmental studies programs to develop sustainability measures such as communal gardens.[64] In Indiana, college students perform the role of mentors to incarcerated juvenile offenders.[65] There are many such examples of openings into a closed penal world for citizens to play a role inside institutions to co-produce something conventional professional practice has failed to deliver; for their part, inmates are beginning their own path back to civic agency.

Third, there is the cultural embarrassment many professionals feel in reproducing an institution that causes human suffering, reflects bitter racial and economic divisions, and generates inequality. This is evident in former attorney general Holder's rhetoric urging his colleagues to be "smarter on crime," noted earlier. With growing awareness of participatory alternatives, as well as greater recognition of institutional weaknesses, comes accountability: the belief that we—professionals and citizens alike—can do better. Though the BPI program might be seen, uncharitably, as the noblesse oblige of one of the most expensive liberal arts colleges in the world, it is also a vibrant sign of accountability—or, as Kenner bluntly states, "Bard believes its own bullshit." Breaking down civic inequality and persistent, chronic divisions is what many went into their professional lives motivated to accomplish. Participatory reforms in criminal justice allow professionals to live up to their own values, to be part of the solution and not the problem.

5

Democratic Innovation in Public Administration

The more we did, the more we were able to do, and the more we were able to do, the more we did.

—VACLAV HAVEL

IN THE LAST decade experiments in democratic innovation have flourished across the country in city and local government agencies in every region, catalyzed by administrators committed to a more active citizenry. On issues such as crime prevention, affordable housing, urban planning, land use and conservation, utility and service provision, and even general budgeting, public participation is actively welcomed in to the work of government. Scholars estimate that thousands of events designed to foster dialogue, generate civic awareness, or make use of community knowledge take place every year in the United States.[1] In the same period public administration professional organizations have bolstered such commitment in their core statements of purpose, in conferences, and in sponsored research. The National League of Cities and the International City/County Management Association, to take two examples, conduct workshops on democratic governance and civic engagement at their annual meetings and disseminate best practices studies and related information. Unlike the cases of criminal justice and K-12 education, commitment to participatory innovation in public administration is overt not covert.

Context and Motivations
The Imperative of Managerialism

While this increase in democratic innovation is encouraging, it has to be put into context. Even reform-minded advocates admit that the dominant mode of professionalism in the field can still be captured by Woodrow Wilson's 1887 characterization in his "The Study of Administration": "The ideal for us is a civil service cultured and self-sufficient enough to act with sense and vigor, and yet so intimately connected with the popular thought, by means of elections and constant public counsel, as to find arbitrariness or class spirit quite out of the question."[2] Wilson was trying to sketch the place of the trained administrator within a democratic constitutional system committed to the principle of popular sovereignty and embedded in a political culture chronically suspicious of government authority. This place was one of the social trustee: the manager earned the public's trust by being "cultured and self-sufficient" and by acting in the public's interests. "Sense and vigor" would be nurtured in professional training where the administrator could acquire specialized knowledge. Responsive to citizens via regular elections and structured public hearings, the administrator was also to be insulated from demotic, factional, partisan, self-interested, short-term pressures of the moment.

Call this Wilsonian social trustee professionalism "managerialism" in order to contrast it with a more substantively democratic model we can label "collaborative." Note that managerialism is not necessarily undemocratic, at least in spirit: it aims to serve the public and pursue common interests, values, and purposes. But the practical means managerialism conceives to serve public interests are, in fact, undemocratic, favoring skilled, knowledgeable, and electorally accountable management over enlisting citizens in collaborating in any way in the work of government. The managerial professional may experiment with the kind of civic innovations emerging in the last decade, but will be reluctant to bring them in to the work of local or municipal government in any significant way.

Reform-minded public administration scholars Larkin Dudley and Ricardo Morse report a persistent "imperative of managerialism" driving public administrators to assume control of situations, take responsibility for certain outcomes, and promote an image of competency.[3] This imperative has three main components, captured in Table 5.1. First is the strict limit placed on transparency: the good public administrator does not share a major problem with the public until he or she already knows the answer to it.[4] Limiting transparency is not just about hiding mistakes, deflecting potential embarrassments, or propping up the image of competency, it is about doing one's job: absorbing the stress and strain of complex issues facing a community, finding a path through conflicting positions on a problem, and working out solutions.

Table 5.1 **Public Administration in Transition?**

	Managerial	Collaborative
Transparency:	Limited	Porous
Authority:	Expert	Shared
Role of Citizen:	Client and Voter	Agent and Resource

A second feature of managerialism is its attitude toward citizens, which is really a working theory of what citizenship entails in a complex society: citizens are clients and voters but not agents in any other respect. Low turnout for local elections? The same familiar faces volunteering for school boards, advisory commissions, and committees? Empty chairs at city council meetings? The managerial standpoint sees these not as signs of any dysfunction but of a community at least modestly satisfied with the performance of its city government. Conflict, controversy, angry citizens showing up by the dozens at public meetings, on the other hand, are signs that some agency, or department, or person is performing poorly. Lay participation in general should be managed so that it turns into support and trust rather than controversy and instability.

Managerialism is characterized, third, by a faith in professional knowledge and training to address administrative problems. This assumption is the foundation of every major professional training program in public administration. Curricula of mainstream programs stress core competencies in budgeting, personnel management, and administrative theory. Community engagement coursework is rare, and concept-rich courses demanding critical thinking about democracy, citizenship, and participation, if offered, are set far off on the periphery of the regular curriculum as electives.[5] Reform-minded faculty at eight leading universities with strong public administration programs were interviewed about institutional commitment to democratic professional ideas. Their narratives are sobering. While democratic citizen engagement enjoys some "few pockets" of support, the faculty reported that mostly "we're on the margins." Worse still, public administration programs appear to be retrenching their managerialism by distancing themselves from democratic symbolism: "Many PA schools used to have words like 'citizenship' and 'public' in the titles, and they've taken them out," one reformer points out. The major accreditation body, National Association for Schools of Public Affairs and Administration, in no way requires training in citizen engagement for accreditation.

Clearly, such faith in managerial professionalism serves the self-interests of programs that must attract fee-paying students—frequently people already working in the public sector but seeking promotions to positions with higher status and greater responsibility. Notice, however, that this faith also follows from personal and institutional commitments to a socially relevant vocation. "I entered public service," remembers former city manager Valerie Lemmie, "because I believed in the power of government to solve society's problems by redistributing resources and stepping in to correct injustices. I couldn't wait to fix problems, ensure good government through improved efficiency and economy, and help people get on with their lives."[6] To gain special knowledge and useful skills that can help others' lives go better is an objective transcending self-interest; achieving such a vocation is a powerful motivator for many who make sacrifices to study, attending night seminars in budgeting, personnel, and organizational structure after a regular eight-hour workday.

So though there is a lot of surface motion trending toward collaboration with citizens, strong currents pull most practitioners back to the status quo, safe harbor of managerialism. As Tina Nabatchi puts it, "Although there has always been (and may always be) an inherent tension in public administration between democratic and bureaucratic ethos, the field has tended to favor and embrace the latter."[7] "When it gets right down to it," Morse echoes, "the old, traditional public administration professionalism ethos tends to still win out more often than not."[8] What we need to explain, then, is this complex dynamic in which there are pressures driving high levels of interest in collaboration, but which only go so far.

Two driving forces of change in particular stand out, and they both threaten the administrator's traditional vocational identity as a social trustee who takes care of public business. The first has to do with what administrators now do, and the second how they communicate with citizens about what they do. The last generation has experienced massive shifts in how governments operate, a time of deep structural reform, shrinking budgets, multifaceted social problems, and changing citizen expectations. In the same period rapid and far-reaching developments in social media and communication have exploded. These forces push administrators toward experimentation, but they also create a kind of conservative pragmatism intensely insecure about efficacy and trust.

Grasping for Efficacy in the New World of Governance

Those entering public administration today encounter a radically different set of institutions than the previous generation occupied. In the 1980s, neoliberal reforms aimed to transform government by shifting a number of traditional agency tasks and public services over to private contractors and, more generally, by broadly and deeply applying market measures of efficiency. These were followed in the 1990s by less radical, but also transformative "new public management" and "new institutionalist" reforms utilizing budgeting and management techniques borrowed from the private sector.[9] The upshot was a mode of "governance" that was less hierarchically organized, relied on non-governmental civil society groups and for-profit private firms to accomplish traditional tasks, and exerted authority via the coordination of horizontal networks of interested organizations and actors. As Mark Bevir puts it,

> contemporary government increasingly involves private- and voluntary-sector organizations working alongside public ones. Complex packages of organizations deliver most public services today. The resulting fragmentation means that the state increasingly depends on other organizations to implement its policies and secure its intentions. Further, the state has swapped direct for indirect controls. Central departments are no longer invariably the fulcrum of policy networks. The state sometimes may set limits to network actions, but it has increased its dependence on other actors. State power is dispersed among spatially and functionally distinct networks.[10]

Scholars of public administration are ambivalent about the results of the last quarter century of reforms, using terms such as "decentered" and "fragmented" to describe government institutions that are no longer on top and no longer hierarchically organized, but now join a number of relevant actors who must coordinate to achieve results. Indeed, such results have been mixed. As Bevir claims, "Neoliberalism may have created a new governance but it was one characterized less by the emergence of properly functioning markets than by the proliferation of networks, the fragmentation of the public sector, and the erosion of central control."[11]

Yet there is a positive side to this decentered and fragmented government landscape, which we have already seen illustrated by Henrik Bang's everyday makers, from Chapter 1. As Bevir also notes, "When the state withdraws—entirely or in part—from the direct provision of a good or service, space for democratic innovations sometimes emerges and substantial forms of collaborative governance and citizen self-organization take root."[12] Indeed, this point should be made with a slightly different emphasis. It is not simply that self-organizing citizens are scrambling forward to occupy the hollowed-out husks left by retreating government agencies. Rather, in some cases proactive democratic professionals are developing new modes of governance within their agencies because they recognize the need to collaborate and help citizens organize to take care of old and new problems. Archon Fung puts this point well, noting that citizens are being brought in to the work of government by public administrators "to address pressing deficits in more conventional, less participatory governance arrangements."[13] Administrators realize they are "somehow deficient," says Fung, lacking in "knowledge, competence, public purpose, resources, or respect necessary to command compliance and cooperation."[14] As social trustee managerialism breaks down, a more democratic form of professionalism begins to look more appealing.

The concerns of working administrators closely reflect the massive shift in the meaning of government in the last generation. Three points are particularly salient. First, managers today are soberly aware of the fiscal limits on their range of action and feel constant pressure to justify their practices in cost-savings terms. As Lemmie notes, "I was being called upon by elected officials to improve government performance, to do more with less and to make our government more customer-service friendly."[15] This pressure hits hardest in urban America, in which city managers "are expected to stimulate economic growth in the face of dwindling federal financial assistance, an eroding tax base, middle-class flight to the suburbs, high rates of poverty and crime, underperforming public schools, aged infrastructure, a precipitous decline in unionized manufacturing jobs, citizen apathy, and elected officials running against 'the bureaucracy.' "[16]

Second, and related, managers are cognizant of the fluid nature of the challenges they face. Their training and knowledge may equip them to handle some aspects of "wicked problems" but they realize they have to collaborate with other professionals, citizen organizations, and active agents with relevant specialized and practical knowledge.[17] "Citizens didn't care about best-management practices," says Lemmie. "They simply wanted their children to play safely in front of their houses. . . . They couldn't understand why what seemed like such a simple thing didn't get done."[18] As Chris Plein has pointed out, public administrators must frequently take up the role of "skilled intermediaries" rather than independent problem-solvers, since issues such as the rural poverty in West Virginia he has spent his career on require close collaboration over time with both people from different professional backgrounds and citizens from affected communities.[19]

A story we can call "The Definition of Insanity" set in Brooklyn Park, Minnesota, illustrates how the pressures of fluid and complex problems can catalyze new ways of conceiving public administration as a shared process. The sixth largest city in Minnesota, Brooklyn Park is the second largest suburb in the Minneapolis metropolitan area. Over the last twenty-five years it underwent significant demographic change. In the 2010 census, neighboring Brooklyn Center was the first minority majority community in Minnesota, with Brooklyn Park right behind at 48 percent nonwhite. It is a diverse community: 20 percent of the population is foreign born, including one of the largest concentration of Liberians living outside the Republic of Liberia.

In the last two decades, Brooklyn Park experienced a dramatic increase in crime, especially in violent crime. The Police Executive Research Forum did a study in 2007, which discovered that about a third of all the crimes committed in the community were being perpetrated by youth and that about a third of all the victims of those crimes were young people as well. So in 2008 city government staff began focused enforcement in problem neighborhoods. While not strictly modeled on New York City's "broken windows" style code enforcement strategy, their approach utilized the same data-driven practices to identify crime hot spots and strategically allocate resources. But despite some early success, violent crime remained a problem. After homicides in 2008 and 2009 involving youth as victims and perpetrators, the mayor and city council members sent a clear message for the police chief and city manager: "This is like the definition of insanity: doing the same thing over and over again and expecting different results. It isn't working. We've got to completely rethink what we're doing."

Brooklyn Park city manager Jamie Verbrugge heard the message and took it as an impetus to shift from a "transactional" to a "transformative" relationship between city government and citizens. "Transactional," for Verbrugge, is a citizen who thinks that paying taxes means getting services; government is in the service delivery business to taxpayer clients. This kind of civic identity may have been encouraged, in part, by managerial-minded public administrators in the past, but in Verbrugge's view it had led to a dead end on problems that require collaboration, or "transformational" relationships to solve. Violent youth crime, he came to see, was just such a problem for Brooklyn Park:

> We had a lot of neighborhood disinvestment. We had a rapid growth
> in the number of single-family residential properties that were

converted to rental properties within neighborhoods already facing
the destabilizing factor of rapid demographic change. You no longer
have the association of long-time neighbors, and then there is this
new element of different races and different cultures and different
ethnicities. That doesn't engender trust. Then you also had transient
populations moving into these communities who lack the motivation of pride of ownership. So you started to see a greater increase
in code enforcement cases. You started to see the properties going
into disrepair—such as chipped or peeled paint, broken windows.
Those are the sorts of things we focused on in the beginning. We
gridded the community based on highest incidence of crime and
code enforcement. We focused on the twenty worst quadrants for
a couple of years through our neighborhood action plan and it was
successful. It dramatically affected those areas. But what we discovered was that the relationship between the city and the service pro-
vider and a service responder was transactional. What we were trying
to get to was a transformational rather than a transactional relationship between the communities and the neighborhoods and the city
staff. Rather than calling the city and expecting us to solve all of their
problems, the idea was to empower neighborhood communities to
become problem solvers on their own. And because of that break-
down in the social compact within neighborhoods we had to rebuild
relationships. And that's why we started the more community-based
effort, to get people away from having the city be the problem-solver
for everything.[20]

Verbrugge, working in tandem with the police chief, developed a collaborative process involving planning and implementation committees composed
of equal numbers of city government staff and residents recruited through
community cafes and other public events. After intense deliberations, the
collaborative group developed a set of core values, a mission statement, and
a set of concrete goals related to youth and diversity, including funding a
teen recreation center and social activities to target the crucial hours between when schools let out and parents come home from work. "We really put together the playbook for how we were going to proceed," says
Verbrugge. "One of the critical pieces was to say that we are going to do
it in partnership with the community. We would have action teams that
were equal part city staff and community members. We would have implementation teams that were equal part staff and community members."[21]

This pattern of one-for-one community advisory bodies grew over the following years to include diversity, budget, and long-term-improvement committees.

Brooklyn Park's experience reflects a third point about contemporary public administration: even when "top-down" management cannot work to solve problems such as youth crime and would not be normatively acceptable to constituents, city managers like Verbrugge are nevertheless still held accountable for service failures. So public engagement turns out to be crucial for sharing information about administrative practice and about the limits of agencies and officials working on their own without community collaboration. "We have too often told citizens . . . that we could supply any service . . . handle all problems at once—and all without raising taxes," says Lemmie. "If there is one aspect to engagement that can lessen tensions and mitigate frustration all around, it is the recognition that we must have priorities in public policy, that we cannot 'do it all' and all at once."[22] As Lynchburg city manager Kimball Payne observes, "it's not the city *and* the citizens or *versus* the citizens or *serving* the citizens, it's all of us working together here. We've got to do this together because we're not given the resources to do this kind of top-down city work. And I'm not sure it's appropriate anyway. So we want them to be involved."[23] Public administrators such as Payne, Lemmie, and Verbrugge desire a broad form of civic education that can take root in a community and help lay citizens to routinely think and act like a city manager—if only periodically. Mere public relations efforts are insufficient for raising awareness of the limits of governance and the complexity of most major problems.

Rebuilding Trust in the Social Media Era

Just as their institutions have undergone major shifts, so has the political culture in which these are embedded. Public administrators today operate in a very different civic landscape than the previous generation, one less connected to the business of government and more wary. Administrators have fewer dependable handholds to get a grip on public interests. Civic engagement in community meetings, local affairs, and neighborhood projects, as well as more formal political participation, has been on a steep decline in the United States since the mid-1970s.[24] As noted earlier, trust in institutions and in fellow citizens—what scholars call vertical and horizontal trust—are at critically low levels. Officials in local and urban government are also impacted by the collateral damage caused by toxic Darwinian national elections with their

breathtaking campaign expenditures, nonstop fundraising, and highly structured and negative debate.

Public administrators are becoming more aware they are part of the
problem they are suffering from. The managerial imperative has fed distrust by
claiming, for generations, professional ownership of public problems: crime,
social order, public health, housing, and educational opportunities.[25] The
new governance model has forced managers into practices that make it obvious that they do not own these problems: they must use private-public
partnerships and other network approaches to do their work. A hands-off approach to the public is no longer possible, yet the habits of managerialism and
the cultural expectations for efficient professional problem-solving persist.

The democratic managers I have interviewed seek to rebuild trust by, first,
frankly admitting they do not have all the answers and, second, conveying to
citizens that they have responsibilities to shoulder if they want good government. As Decatur city manager Andrea Arnold observes, "we believe strongly
that our citizens should be involved and we want them involved in problem
solving, decision making, making planning decisions, and ultimately having
them take some action to make improvements in the community. It is not just
they vote to elect someone and then we carry it out." Arnold's perspective
is a mixture of civic idealism and hardheaded pragmatism: "I think it's okay
for us to say that we in city government do not have all the good ideas," she
says, insisting, "we would be remiss in not tapping into the resources in our
community. We could have the resources, the brainpower, of two hundred
city employees or we can have that collectively at twenty thousand people.
We have some amazing volunteers out here who have an expertise in development, storm water, trees, traffic, engineering—a wealth of experience and
knowledge that we could not otherwise pay for."[26]

Posing additional challenges to trust are the commercial and technolog-
ical changes in media and communications. Rising costs and declining pa-
tronage forced a wave of consolidations in the 1980s and continue to press
American news-media organizations toward leaner operations with fewer
reporters. To remain competitive, news-media favor coverage of fast-breaking
stories, dramatic events, and personality-rich narratives over slower news
stories about policy issues and official decisions or in-depth investigative journalism. Further applying pressure to old media such as newspapers are rapid
developments in new online media: aggregators culling—and often mixing—
traditional journalism, opinion, and lay information from global sources,
Facebook, Twitter, Instagram, and many others. Not only do people have
exactly the information they want when they want it, they have the ability

to share their own information and opinions with others, everywhere, instantly. As with the world of government, the new media world is decentered and fragmented, but it has also opened different and sometimes surprisingly robust ways of connecting officials with citizens. As Nabatchi observes, "although citizens have withdrawn from traditional civic and political activities, the advent of the Internet and other digital technologies has stimulated new citizen attitudes and engagement capacities."[27]

Declining citizen trust produces instability and unpredictability for city managers. While more secure in their offices than their elected colleagues, political upheavals can threaten managers by disrupting continuity in planning and policy implementation. In this negatively charged political environment, new media innovations have both empowered and agitated citizens. The civic playing field today is incredibly "touchy" and sensitive to things going wrong. In the "good old days," observes Kim Payne, "you just have a formal public meeting and then make the decision you think best for the community and move on. But with today's social media and instant communication, I think you really need folks in the community who know what is going on, are involved, and feel like they're part of the process."[28] New media are viewed as a goad, on the one hand, but also as platforms to reach out and tell people the city manager's side of the story, to listen but also to educate. When he began work as a public administrator, Payne notes, "I did not have to deal with Facebook or Twitter or any of these social media. When someone comes into city hall . . . and has a bad interaction and they walk out the door and tweet and put it on Facebook, now a thousand people know about it. The world has really changed on us. You have to listen to these folks; you have to treat them with respect; you have to help them to understand where they just misunderstand, but you really need to have these conversations."[29]

Types of Substantive Citizen Involvement in Public Administration
Ad Hoc Strategies

All of the prolonged commitments to public participation I encountered in my interviews and background research began with specific projects formed in direct response to a pressing problem typically connected to a chronic, complex, and emotional issue such as race, crime, violence, property rights, and neighborhood control. To solve the problem, no simple administrative or purely political answer was possible. Wider resources were required: greater community awareness and citizen agency had to be added to the professional skills already involved.

In late summer 2006, for example, the City of Lynchburg was facing the kind of deeply rooted questions of race and policing that would flare up nationally and more prominently a decade later. A forty-six-year old black resident, Clarence Beard, had died in police custody under murky circumstances. "In the wake of the tragic incident," the Lynchburg *News and Advance* reported, "accusations of police brutality and of a whitewash investigation arose in the black community, exposing an ugly tear in the social fabric of the city."[30] The city, which is roughly two-thirds white and one-third black, had to come to grips with some sober truths about racial division.

Realizing that mainstream public relations techniques would not suffice, city manager Payne, working closely with the mayor, Joan Foster, and community leaders, decided that the city government had to find a way to listen as well as speak. They settled on a participatory public process involving community forums and study circles. Groups of eight to twelve members convened for six weeks, meeting two hours every week. Their open-ended discussions aimed to work through the issue and form an agenda for community action. By the end of 2008, over 1,300 citizens had joined the conversation. Now known as Many Voices One Community, this program is an ongoing and self-sustaining effort in public education, involvement, and advocacy around issues of race and racism.

The community dialogue prompted improvements in diversity training within the Lynchburg Police Department, generated initiatives designed to increase workforce diversity in city government and area businesses, and started the groundwork for a college scholarship program. Like the experience with citizen advisory committees in Brooklyn Park, citizen participation came to be an expected part of Lynchburg city government, with study circles and other forms of dialogue frequently used to evaluate budget priorities and provide input on city planning. What began as a modus vivendi is now a way of public life.

I call such innovations "ad hoc strategies" because they are directed at a single problem, but note that they are well structured. In Lynchburg following the death of Clarence Beard in police custody, Payne and Mayor Foster deliberately turned to the study circle format to transcend the limits of traditional "three minutes at the microphone" public meetings. As Payne notes, "we realized we didn't want a typical formal public meeting where people stand up and fuss, but that probably won't accomplish much. What we needed was a *discussion*. We needed to have some real dialogue, which involves people really listening and hearing what others are saying and then reacting to that in an environment that is safe and protected for all the participants."[31]

Ad hoc forums designed to foster community dialogue require dedicated organizers who seek out creative ways of involving those residents who typically stay on the sidelines. In Lynchburg, Payne's staff worked closely with more active community members to bring less-involved people into the process:

> It was very much more than the usual suspects. We formed a steering committee of interested citizens and city staff folks. We spent probably close to a year just planning for this discussion. And even within those planning meetings we formed some relationships with the people involved. And we said we wanted to have 1000 people involved. We set that as an audacious goal. We really tried to reach out beyond the normal situation where you advertise a public hearing and a few regulars show up. We tried to work with the local sororities and fraternities in the African American community. We tried to reach out to the Hispanic community, to the Korean community, to anybody who would listen to us to try to get the word out.[32]

The need to be proactive and ask citizens to be involved is a consistent finding that extends across every type of substantive participatory innovation in public administration.[33] Managers find it insufficient just to build a forum, publicize it, and hope people attend; the successful democratic innovators make it a priority to recruit citizens, provide incentives, and, to use Verbrugge's well-chosen words, "to take people's excuses away." Frequently, reform-minded city managers will bring someone on to the staff who can serve as a "community coordinator," rather than add volunteer recruitment and forum facilitation to the responsibilities of current public employees.

Effective ad hoc forums deliberate and in doing so create a more reflective public discussion about the issue at hand, one more aware of the history of an issue such as race and racism, the personal stakes people have in the problem, and the resources available in the community to deal with it. Yet these forums are not just talk: they produce outcomes. One outcome of an effective ad hoc forum is relationship building among active citizens and city government staff, and among citizens themselves:

> We discovered some people we didn't know before who have since become leaders in the community. People formed relationships; they met

people in the study circle process they never would have crossed paths with in their normal day-to-day occurrences. A prominent white businessman and an older black woman, for example, told me they still communicate with each other. They acknowledge that they look at the world from entirely different perspectives but they became friends through the process. I mean, there are not hundreds of those stories, but each of them is pretty heartwarming.[34]

There can also be concrete policy outcomes to such a process. As noted, in Lynchburg, the study circles prompted changes in policing as well as city initiatives related to race. Such initiatives continue the process of collaboration between residents and city government staff, observes Payne: "We have a group that is working to provide college scholarships for students who need them to get into higher education—called Beacon of Hope. That was a direct outgrowth of the study circle process."[35]

Ad hoc forums address specific issues, but they can also become sustainable and stay together to deal with the same issue over time. In Lynchburg, the dialogues on race and racism have continued because of ground-level citizen organizing. "Many Voices One Community . . . are still meeting," notes Payne, "They formed a board of directors. They don't get a lot of support from the city other than encouragement. And they actually held a seminar this fall over a Saturday and got about eighty people who came and discussed issues of race and racism. And that group is still sponsoring study circles too."[36] Effective ad hoc forums can also catalyze the development of other forums. Following the success of "Many Voices," Lynchburg city government has used study circles for road planning, comprehensive plan dialogues, budget discussions, and a host of other community meetings.

The Civic Umwelt: An Environmental Commitment to Participation

The German word "Umwelt," meaning "world around," conveys a concrete geographical demarcation of the local streets, neighborhoods, and terrain of a town as well as the feeling of the close awareness of the things and people we are most likely to experience regularly. When a town has a multitude of ad hoc forums and there is intentionality behind this proliferation we can say there is a "civic Umwelt," or an environmental commitment to participation. Some democratic city managers cultivate a participatory culture by organizing or supporting lots of events all the time.

The work of city managers Peggy Merriss and Andrea Arnold in Decatur, Georgia, is a good example. As in Lynchburg, Virginia, Decatur has used study circles run by trained volunteer facilitators for broad community discussions of strategic city planning. Called Decatur Round Tables, these emerged in the process of developing the city's year 2000 strategic plan through a collaboration with long-time community organizer Jon Abercrombie, who was concerned about affordable housing in a rapidly gentrifying city.[37] Ten years later, the Round Tables were incorporated into the next phase of strategic planning and involved more than 1,500 residents in town meetings, expert presentations, and facilitated small-group discussions designed to develop core principles and implementable objectives. The Round Tables, held over the course of two months, demanded significant commitment on the part of participants, as noted by Decatur staff: "There were three Round Table sessions. Each session comprised of 11 separate meetings held at different times and places around the city. The first session involved 741 citizens, the vast majority of whom (78 percent) returned for the second and third sessions." All told, "participants offered 7,894 ideas and images about Decatur's current situation, possible future, and issues facing the city."[38]

Decatur Round Tables became embedded, moreover, in an intentionally created participatory environment involving multiple points of contact among citizens, experts, and officeholders. "We would have," says Arnold, "what we called academy sessions where experts come out and provide their professional expertise input on the subject matter. We were using Facebook and Twitter to keep people updated on the progress of the plan. We had these meetups at coffee shops—you might get a text, 'This morning at ten o'clock we're going to have a meetup at Starbucks. Drop by and give us your feedback on this part of the planning process.'"[39] In addition to the study circle process and informal meetups, city government now organizes a five-day citizens' academy called Decatur 101, in which citizens meet with officials and learn about administrative services, budgeting, and other elements of the business of government.

There is not one single "signature" forum in Decatur, just many experiments. Indeed, not all of the community events that make up the civic Umwelt are political. Arnold's department helps organize cultural events such as book, arts, beer, and wine festivals with an eye on more than just some good weekend fun:

> [P]eople come out and have a good time, but there is also a method
> behind this too. We have a volunteer coordinator who recruits people

to help with these festivals. Probably one of the best decisions we ever made was to hire someone whose sole job is to corral volunteers, which is not an easy task. So you get people engaged doing this kind of work supporting these events so they get to know each other, they get to know their neighbors. It is all good and well. Everyone's happy at the beer festival. But then when there are really serious and contentious issues, like the development moratorium, and people are coming out with their concerns, those relationships have been built and that trust has been built. I would say it is about connecting people [and] building trust within the community and so you engage folks in a positive way and then when there are tough times or tough issues you have that trust in place. Whereas in some cities you see that people are completely disengaged and then what happens when there is some controversial issue? They come out, they have no level of trust in these people that have been elected, and it is not normally a very pretty experience. So . . . I would say there is a *deliberateness* about the community events.[40]

Purely cultural or hedonistic events still lead to civic networking useful for the "serious" work later on.

Events that in less pervasively active communities can be superficial or transient become enriched in towns with a civic Umwelt by the deeper connections they achieve. The three-day Martin Luther King Day weekend in Decatur, for example, involves large-scale community service projects in which local contractors and developers take charge of specific houses needing repair, donate time and materials, and help organize citizen volunteer workers. City government is not the prime actor, but does contribute staff labor and some resources to what is a community-initiated project. "We will identify homes within the community—normally lower income, elderly people who have had trouble maintaining their homes, whether it is yard work, or simple repairs, or not so simple repairs. A lot of them just did not want to ask for help. But again, we have the relationships that are built up in the community and we find out that Ms. Smith does not have running water at her house or the lights are out."[41] These sorts of events bring people together who may not have wanted to be together. They spread out some degree of responsibility for major social problems—eldercare, poverty, neighborhood disrepair, and in so doing nurture an alert and supportive culture. The upshot for the citizen is a community worth living in. For the public administrator, an additional benefit is the more constructive change in tone in formal meetings. "It is not uncommon," says Arnold, "for there to be something controversial on our agendas, but when people are at the meetings they are civil and respectful and a lot of communities cannot say that. And I think it is because these are people who have worked shoulder to shoulder in some other capacity or they know someone who has."[42]

Along with promoting and supporting "high touch" face-to-face events such as study circle forums, cultural festivals, and service projects, Decatur administrators experiment with "high tech" modes of connecting citizens to each other and to the work of government. Arnold develops online surveys, keeps up with social media, and uses technology such as Open City Hall to hold virtual meetings.

> We will periodically put up questions on Open City Hall and ask people to chime in. For example, recently we were looking at making changes to a tree protection ordinance so we asked questions about that. While we worked on the ordinance, the City Commission approved a ninety-day moratorium on tree removal. During this ninety-day period we met with stakeholders such as property owners, developers, and real estate agents. Also, the City's Environmental Sustainability Board, which is made up of community volunteers appointed by the City Commission, was engaged to provide input for the ordinance. In addition to these public meetings, just prior to the public hearing, we placed the proposed ordinance and supporting documentation on Open City Hall and asked people if they supported the adoption of the proposed ordinance. We received five hundred and sixty-four comments, which were provided to the City Commissioners. After hearing from the public, the City Commission is now in the process of modifying the proposed ordinance. We put the budget out there every year on Open City Hall and people can vote yes or no on whether they like this or not and provide their feedback. Motivating this use of technology is our understanding that for a lot of people, coming to a city commission meeting at 7:30 on a Monday night is not the most convenient thing for our different lifestyles. So you have an option to participate in that way.[43]

The civic *Umwelt* of a city such as Decatur makes it hard for citizens to avoid true public spaces: sites to meet, talk, and solve problems together. While no specific forum or process dominates, taken together they generate a cultural expectation of responsibility. A recursiveness is at work: being involved in

Decatur is easy, fun, and meaningful. As you become involved in one sort of event, you form connections that encourage further involvement. Indeed, you may be called on again and again by community organizations or city government: "You have gotten your foot in the door because you attended the arts festival. You volunteered for the beach party. Or you went to Decatur 101 and you are on our mailing list." The democratic city manager makes opportunities available and constantly reaches out to pull people in: "I think you have a job as a citizen to be involved and to be engaged. And we need to give you the opportunity to be involved and engaged."[44]

Educational Innovations: Citizens' Academies

One part of Decatur's civic Umwelt, the civic education program called Decatur 101, is an example of another recent democratic innovation, the citizens' academy. While meant primarily as a means of informing citizens about city government and therefore not intended as a way of sharing power or collaborating, citizens' academies are significant because they can hold open government work to inspection, make officials available to citizens, and encourage a robust form of citizenship for future power-sharing and collaboration.

In practice for over a decade, Decatur 101 has enrolled nearly a thousand community members in a hands-on public education experience. Arnold explains how it works and what it offers citizens and city managers.

> You sign up for Decatur 101 and you commit to five or six meetings, either mornings or evenings. So when you come out on my evening, it is going to be administrative services, personnel, budget. You come out to city hall. You meet my staff and me. We talk about what we do, why we do it, and who we are. Then we have a really fun budget exercise they participate in. It is all good and well that they are learning what we do, but what we hear from people who go through this is they say they are most impressed when they see how much we—their public employees—love our jobs: we love what we do, we are extremely competent. These people do not really know what they are getting into. Their neighbor told them to take Decatur 101 and then they go through and they have learned a tremendous amount about their community. And they become our biggest supporters and spokespeople when they are out in the neighborhood. And when some issue comes up they can say, "Oh well, I was at that class and here's the real story" or

"This is who you need to call about it." So I would say that is another way that we get people engaged. This is about us providing information and making ourselves available.[45]

Payne organizes a citizens' academy in Lynchburg and talks in similar terms about the benefits of transparency, public awareness, and trust.

[Our] Citizens' Academy is an 11-week program that enrolls about thirty people a year. They visit all the different city departments and facilities and learn about how and why we do things. To a person they usually come out of it saying, "I had no idea. You guys are doing a great job." And they become advocates in the community. We get volunteers from the Academy. We get people who serve on boards and commissions from it and we have actually gotten some city council members too.

Citizens' academies are relatively new, having emerged in the 1990s, but share family resemblances with other kinds of civic education programs with longer histories, such as citizen police academies and community leadership programs. Like the former, they are sponsored by local government and are open to any interested citizen, and like the latter they cover a range of topics. They are increasingly common on the ground: one recent study of citizens' academies in North Carolina found them in nearly a quarter of all counties with populations over 100,000.[46] In some cities, such as Hampton Virginia, where they are called "Neighborhood Colleges," their primary focus is to develop community leaders and long-term citizen volunteers.[47]

Citizens' academies typically demand a significant investment of time from participants—five weeks of meetings in Decatur, for example, and eleven weeks in Lynchburg. In North Carolina, academies average twenty hours of instruction time spread out over a number of weeks. Programs are heavily oriented toward hands-on learning and typically take participants on tours of city government offices, fire and police departments, water treatment facilities, and other places where the work of government gets done. Operated at very low cost, citizens' academies recruit participants by aiming for a fun, enriching experience.

The stated goals of citizens' academies are clear: to increase citizen knowledge of local government, to involve citizens in local government, and to improve relations between local government with the community. These goals, however, can be approached superficially—with academies serving merely as public relations campaigns for agencies and officials—or they can be part of a more substantive effort of democratic professionals to encourage the kind of robust knowledge and awareness among citizens that will serve as a solid foundation for future collaboration.[48]

Power-Sharing Innovations: Participatory Budgeting

A collaborative practice combining the educational opportunities of citizens' academies with a functional, power-sharing role, is participatory budgeting. Prominently associated with the Brazilian city of Porto Alegre, where organized work groups of citizens have been annually allocating around 20 percent of the city budget since 1989, participatory budgeting has grown rapidly over the last decade in the United States.[49] Major cities such as Boston, Chicago, New York City, San Francisco, Seattle, and St. Louis have experimented with this process. The most extensive use in this country has been in the cities of Chicago, where participatory budgeting spread from one district in 2009 to nine in 2017, and New York City, where the process grew from four districts in 2011 to thirty-one districts just six years later.[50] While the funds allocated can be substantial ($38 million in New York City), these are often a tiny fraction of the city's budget ($80 billion in the case of New York City). The process has spread outside major metropolitan areas as well, with smaller cities and towns intentionally integrating citizen participation in budgeting in ways that borrow from the Brazilian model while adapting to fit local circumstances and innovating to target specific populations. In Boston, for example, the mayor's office developed a "Youth Lead the Change" process in which young people are charged with deciding how to make use of a $1 million portion of the budget.

An early adopter was Chicago's 49th Ward, where Alderman Joe Moore set aside $1.3 million of his discretionary budget to be allocated through participatory budgeting. He invited leaders of community groups to be part of a steering committee and, in the following months, held neighborhood assemblies to draw out participants and to generate budget priorities. Representatives from these assemblies then formed six work committees devoted to specific issues, such as the Public Safety Committee and the Transportation Committee. Over a four-month period, in consultation with experts in their problem area, the committees researched, deliberated, and developed concrete budget proposals. The Public Safety Committee, for example, had to decide whether to prioritize funding for security cameras or streetlights, so they toured the camera-monitoring center and met with police to discuss which was more effective. Then, after another round of neighborhood assemblies to discuss each committee's budget proposals, a ballot emerged containing thirty-six budget proposals. The ballot was exhibited prominently at community organizations and cultural centers with the notification that soon all ward residents above the age of sixteen would have a chance to vote on it. The resulting vote generated support for fourteen of the top budget proposals, which gained a portion of the $1.3 million. Fixing sidewalks was the top vote getter, with bike lanes, street lighting, traffic signals, and community gardens also earning citizens' support.[51]

What motivates public administrators and other officials to share power over such a specialized and often conflict-ridden process? Porto Alegre turned to participatory budgeting following Brazil's transition from authoritarian government; city officials sought new processes to learn directly from the most marginalized populations about their interests and to gain their practical insights regarding the most efficacious use of public funds for meeting community needs. Previous technocratic government efforts had failed to reach these citizens, so participatory budgeting was utilized as a method of organizing and empowering their voices within a hitherto closed-off decision-making process. In Chicago, Alderman Moore took up participatory budgeting after a narrow election indicated he needed to find new ways of getting in touch with 49th Ward residents; he began to realize that the closed door practices of managerialism were contributing to distrust and apathy among his constituents.[52] In other cities, too, administrators are drawn to participatory budgeting to regain trust during difficult times, as the City of Vallejo, California, did after declaring bankruptcy during the Great Recession, or to find the most publicly acceptable ways to cut desired programs and services during lean years, as the City of Hampton, Virginia, did in the same period. It is a way of proactively narrowing the distance between officials and citizens, especially those citizens on the margins of public life and those most likely to be affected by cuts in programs and services.[53]

Like citizens' academies and ad hoc participatory forums and round tables, participatory budgeting procedures also help achieve greater social proximity between citizens themselves. Reform advocate Josh Lerner calls it a "giant community-building and community-organizing process," one that "uses money as a carrot to get people engaged in powerful new ways."[54] During a participatory budgeting process in New York City, for example, a teacher serving as a member of an Education Committee began as a firm proponent of a budget proposal seeking funding for an outdoor teaching space for his middle school. While researching the other schools in his district, however, he discovered more pressing needs, such as the missing doors in the girls' bathrooms in one elementary school. Setting his own school's needs aside, he told a reporter, "Now I'm arguing for some complete strangers' toilets."[55] As Lerner puts it, "there is a deeper, qualitative impact of face-to-face engagement: transformative learning. By engaging in months of focused discussions and field research with diverse residents from all walks of life, participants often transform their views of both the community and themselves."[56]

In the cities where this process is expanding, administrators and officials interested in reconnecting with citizens appear to be met more than halfway by residents glad to have a voice outside the ballot box and by civic organizations drawn upon as essential structural components—useful conduits for information, experience, tools, rulebooks, and other materials necessary to encourage participation. Though research on the efficacy of the process in the United States is still scant, early studies suggest it does reach people previously uninterested in participation. In Chicago, a majority of those active in the process reported "no or little previous involvement in civic activities and organizations."[57] In New York City, participatory budgeting attracted people under the age of twenty-five at a significantly higher rate than traditional local elections; though more demanding than attending a public hearing or voting, the process was experienced by many as a valuable civic skills building exercise.[58] There are signs of the recursiveness noticed in other forms of democratic innovation: the more public administrators and officials trust citizens and the greater the sense citizens have about their civic efficacy, the more hopeful they are about government even when their own favored budget proposal fails to win enough of their neighbors' support. "PB is a happy space," noted one active resident of Chicago's 10th Ward, "because it's a productive space. This is where we work on solving our problems."[59]

Long Haul Institutional Commitments

Some democratic professional city managers encourage regular citizen involvement in procedures such as participatory budgeting as a natural part of "doing business" and something to be invested in for the long haul. Four main factors seem to be relevant to the successful embedding of citizen engagement. First is *division of labor*. Not every topic, issue, problem, or decision is suitable for collaboration. It is important to avoid the practical, routine, or technical items government is expected to handle as a matter of course and to focus on general problem or policy areas citizens need to weigh in on. Lynchburg City Manager Payne explains:

I don't think I could get much public enthusiasm about running a wastewater treatment plant. But on some of the budget choices we make on what sort of service delivery mixes we have, for example, they're not going to question *how* we deliver the services as much as whether it is an appropriate service to be delivered and how it should be paid for. And those are issues I'm really not sure there is a professional answer to. Again, I can deliver water all day long, but should we privatize the water system? That's a broader and a more policy-oriented question. How dynamic should our parks and recreation system be? Are we willing to sacrifice parks and recreation for public education or for public safety?

We're dabbling a little bit with priority-based budgeting and I think those sorts of discussions about our priorities—what is important to this community—those are the things that you take to the citizens. I don't think how we run the bus system is something they really care about. They do care when we cut service though![60]

Division of labor is a loose concept and admits of a great deal of flexibility and openness to change over time. The democratic professionals I have interviewed learn by doing what works to bring citizens into the work of government in a productive way and what does not.

A second main factor in successfully embedding citizen participation is *relentless outreach*. As noted earlier, democratic public administrators take away excuses not to participate. In Lynchburg, Decatur, Hampton, and Brooklyn Park, they meet where the people are. As Verbrugge puts it, "if you really want to get to where people are, first of all you have to *go* to where they are. You have to go to the youth groups, the sports clubs, the social organizations; you have to go to the churches."[61] As a democratic city manager from Fort Collins, Colorado, observes, "We resource the heck out of our community engagement. We spend a lot of time, a lot of money and a lot of FTEs."[62] Equally important, city staff try to operate on citizens' timetables, scheduling meetings right after work but before dinner, or making it easy to chime in on a discussion online or at a cafe before work. Finally, they make it an imperative, broadcasting throughout their organization the need to devote time and human resources to citizen engagement. Successfully embedded engagement demands deep commitment on the part of city managers and their staff. It is not enough just to build spaces or hold forums; engagement requires proactive work.

A third factor in long haul institutional commitment is what people are doing once they are recruited. They are meeting with other citizens and officials and they are talking, but they are also doing *substantive work*. There are outcomes to their involvement; they make a difference to their community by showing up. Engagement is not just symbolic of a good community and a receptive government; engagement helps make a community good and a government receptive. Civic engagement helped untangle a wicked youth crime problem in Brooklyn Park, constructively confronted racial trust issues between white police and black citizens in Lynchburg, helped unravel a knotty problem of affordable housing in gentrifying Decatur, and helped identify highly specific community needs in neighborhoods across New York City, Chicago, Boston, and elsewhere. Substantive work, done collaboratively, clears a network of trails for citizens and administrators to follow on future projects.

Fourth and finally, institutional commitment means establishing real *power-sharing* places for citizens—on committees, boards, or lay offices—whether these are seats at decision-making tables or significant contributing roles in longer-term planning or implementation processes. In Dayton, Lemmie worked with institutionalized citizen councils called Priority Boards, set up to deal with neighborhood complaints.[63] In Brooklyn Park, Verbrugge established citizen problem-solving teams on the topics of resources, diversity, and youth to advise his fellow officials. Such positions require skillful planning on the part of public administrators; while citizens resent being given only small bore tasks and purely symbolic busywork, if positions are made into quasi-official roles, these can sometimes become part of the entrenched institutionalized world they are meant to open up, so care must be taken to avoid what Lemmie calls "citizen-bureaucrats."[64]

Growth and Sustainability

To move beyond shallow commitments to lay participation, all these long-term strategies seem to be necessary. Over time, however, it is the everyday maker, the organized citizen group, and the community that will reinforce democratic professionalism when managerialism begins to crop back up. Here we return to the concept of recursiveness: successful long-term participatory innovation develops a creative dynamic that begins to have a life of its own. Payne tells an important story:

We had a council meeting last week that included a public hearing about AT&T's plan to erect a cell tower in a residential neighborhood. Boy, the neighbors came out for that one. And these are folks we would not normally see attend anything. They came out in full force, spoke, went through the public hearing process, and certainly had their voices heard. The issue got tabled for further analysis and more work. The interesting thing is that AT&T had not talked to the community prior to appearing before council. A number of these folks said, "Why didn't you come and talk to us?" So there is this expectation now. We will do that if we have an initiative: we will go into the neighborhood and talk to people. This company had not done that and they really got criticized.[65]

At some point there is no turning back to business as usual.

6

Growing and Sustaining Cultures of Participatory Innovation: Barriers, Openings, and the Role of Democratic Inquiry

When I start looking at walls, I begin to see the writing.
—SAMUEL BECKETT

WHY WOULD CREATING a participatory budgeting process, a prison discussion group, or a conflict-resolution program for a 5th-grade classroom matter, if most decision-making in educational, governmental, and criminal justice institutions proceeds in a relatively non-participatory fashion? In small, medium, and large ways, citizens can become load-bearing members of our public institutions, and in so doing help them work and think and act differently.

Sparks of Democratic Energy among Professionals

Democratic professionals bring laypeople together to make justice, education, public health, city government, and the like as a regular part of the social environment. For these reformers, institutions are fields of democratic action produced by citizens acting together; they encourage and regulate action, to be sure, but they are not fixed forms. Yet what keeps innovators going when they hit obstacles or when resources needed to support their work dry up? How are others encouraged to take up similar projects?

What is fascinating but perhaps unsurprising is that the personal histories of many democratic professionals I have met reflect intense pessimism and disaffection with contemporary institutions. The schools, agencies, and programs for which they received work training appear to be controlled by untouchable forces of bureaucracy and managerialism. Moreover, these institutions seem to be failing to produce the services and outcomes they promise or to treat people well as citizens and human beings. Interviewees said that their traditional training set them up to be successful failures. They recognized that being the best conventional professional they could be was insufficient to rectify the problems plaguing these domains; and while this could have easily led to apathy, quietism, and careerism, it did not for them. The fighting creed of the democratic professional is the absolute refusal to perpetuate the dysfunctions of the currently dominant institutional environment. I have heard this sentiment expressed in numerous ways: *I refuse to reproduce schools, administrative offices, and government programs that do things* to *rather than* with *people, that disempower, that devalue or discourage lay contributions, that frustrate collaboration, that hinder collective work. I have one life, and with it, I will make my school, my office, my program a place of agency, of sharing, of dignity.*

Forest Grove principal Vanessa Gray helped create a democratic school because she did not want to reproduce the institutional patterns of two other schools in her district. The high school is like a prison, she said, with a metal detector at the entrance and security cameras everywhere. In the elementary school, kids late to class are inked with a hand stamp in the image of a tortoise.[1] Gray was not going to perpetuate a school culture that failed to treat people with dignity, as anything less than full citizens of the society they'd soon enter. "On graduation day," notes democratic principal George Wood, "when I shake the hands of graduates, I am welcoming them into our community as neighbors and peers. They now step forward to run our stores, take care of the elderly and the young, vote on tax levies. . . . It is only when we see high school graduates in this light, as our equals, that we will seriously rethink how we treat them in school."[2]

A related factor is complexity and the absurdity of declaring professional jurisdiction over tasks traditionally claimed by social trustee forebears. This is clear in the "wicked problems" public administrators talk about: the policy areas such as substance abuse, urban poverty, and homelessness, which require a multifaceted—and indeed highly democratic—kind of professional collaboration to adequately comprehend, define, and address. Yet it is increasingly clear that all traditional professional tasks are wicked in their own ways, as profession after profession is forced by circumstance to admit their limited grasp on complex problems: health requires not just good medical care but sound nutrition, which requires the elimination of food deserts; public safety requires not just good policing but communities attentive to broken windows and the lack of after-school youth activities; and on it goes. While it is still all too easy to respond to complexity by shoring up the symbols of social trustee professionalism and doubling down on managerial attitudes, declarations of vulnerability and invitations to collaborate appear commonly in the stories practitioners tell one another in professional meetings and training workshops about successful problem-solving.

Barriers and Openings to Democratic Professionalism

Whether we are lay citizens, professionals, or professionals in training, we can each play a role in growing cultures of participatory innovation where we live and work. Our task will be helped along by sober recognition of both the obstacles in the path of innovations and some of the sources of support available along the way. Both barriers and openings for democracy exist in most professionalized domains.

As we've seen, democratic agency has some powerful barriers, noted in Table 6.1. Changes made by democratic professionals are more retail in nature than the wholesale changes sought by traditional social movement activists, yet they are not minor achievements. They manage to swim against some very strong counter-democratic currents: bureaucratic demands for efficiency, cost control, and clear chains of command; legal constraints that carve out specific zones of authority and responsibility; and economic incentives to assert jurisdictional control over certain problems, issues, and tasks.

Table 6.1 Barriers and Openings for Democracy in Professionalized Domains

Barriers	Openings
Jurisdictional claims of professions	"Wicked" cross-profession problems
Authority, responsibility, obligation	Division of labor and shared responsibility
Expertise	Local and social knowledge
Hierarchy and efficiency	Release of individual and group capacity

Practitioners find opportunities for change as well as resources and allies. So-called wicked problems such as youth violence, which admit no unidimensional expert response, can prompt otherwise risk-averse criminal justice professionals to collaborate with community members. Fixed and centralized government authority is given a reason to relax when participatory processes yield results by using local problem-solving knowledge. Hierarchy in schools, when it dampens students' powerful curiosity, sense of wonder, and love of inquiry, as many democratic teachers have discovered, can also loosen its organizational hold. More generally, too, widespread resentment of invasive, autonomy-threatening managerialism among skilled professionals motivates strategically useful allies in democratic culture change in a school, agency, program, or department.

Participatory democracy has a major strategic advantage, too. These practitioners are enacting changes at the local and institutional levels that can improve lives immediately. By circumventing the slow wheels of legal or political machinery, their participatory innovations enable children to learn in more responsive schools, neighbors to take part in inclusionary community justice efforts, and prisoners to interact as citizens right away. Students, neighbors, and inmates improve their well-being at the very moment they conduct their work. Their collaborative, reflective, and at times load-bearing work can itself be a valuable end result.

Participatory innovation does not emerge naturally, accidentally, or spontaneously; it is part of many quiet struggles inside relatively closed institutions. As we have noticed, for example, in American K-12 education student participation in norm setting and adjudication is, in the words of student voice advocate Dana Mitra, "counternormative." Much more common is the top-down approach of the principal applying the rule and meting out a sanction. The ongoing struggle between these modes comes to the surface in debates over the hardening of school disciplinary sanctions against student norm-breakers and in discussions of alternative procedures such as restorative justice. Seemingly trivial and all-too-local from the perspective of traditional democratic theory, these are the small battles that will define future institutions as fields of self-government or will continue to reproduce the repellent status quo. Thus, more attention needs to be paid to what citizens, academics, and fellow practitioners might do to sustain and encourage people such as Vanessa Gray, Kim Payne, Lauren Abramson, and many other innovators on the inside and outside of institutions who are making them more reflective and participatory.

It is commonplace to assert against arguments like mine that widespread lay participation is somehow too idealistic for the real world of heterogeneous publics and complex policy problems. Yet, in fact, I have found that collaboration and power-sharing efforts are frequently initiated when the going gets tough for city managers, school district leaders, and police chiefs. They find, in times of crisis, that rationally disorganized institutions are the way to regain public trust after a budget shortfall, police shooting, or school performance failure. It is the expert institution, sealed off from the public it is meant to serve, that is too pure for this modern world. Participatory innovators may be idealists, but they are also realists; they know the humanizing practices they seek to bring into currently closed and repellent institutional spaces are desperately needed in the real world.

There is a long way to go, of course, though it helps to think of participatory democracy not as a specific achievable goal, technique, model, or set of best practices but as a range of ongoing, open-ended, always-imperfect paths and settlements as human beings move along and seek to work out their problems together. There are different kinds of imperfect, too; not every participatory innovation should be embraced by those who care about democracy. In describing practical forms of citizen involvement in previously professionalized domains, we also need to evaluate the collaborative tasks and degree of power-sharing that are emerging, and reject the sham and the symbolic.

Navigating between "Best Practices" and the "Hermeneutics of Suspicion"
Divergent Paths of Analysis and Evaluation

To better assess openings and barriers to participatory democracy today and to understand what those of us who work with ideas and words might contribute to supporting practical efforts at innovation, we need to attend to the ways we construct concepts and arguments—both descriptive and normative. My thinking on democratic innovation has benefited from many qualitative case studies in the fields of education, criminal justice, and public administration. Yet in making use of these studies I have been struck by the ways they often reflect, in a methodological fashion, the proceduralist and pessimistic strands of democratic theory noted in Chapter 1. An odd disjuncture exists between optimistic "best practices" case studies and a highly critical body of work I call the "hermeneutics of suspicion."[3] While the former offers how-to advice for future practitioners, the latter cautions any would-be innovator to take care because underneath the surface phenomenon of a so-called "best practice"—whether it is a study circle, citizen forum, or civic roundtable—lurk counter-democratic forces that can neutralize citizen agency.

Because they often focus on the mechanics of participatory innovation, best practices studies help identify just what it takes to have robust demo-cratic conversations about social problems. Well-crafted studies describe living, breathing human beings who have made—sometimes significant—sacrifices of time and resources to create innovative programs.[4] And the prag-matic, future-oriented methodological stance characteristic of best practices scholarship is, on its own terms at least, unassailable. These scholars straight-forwardly present cases they believe others can learn from, modify, and use to contribute to widespread democratic innovation. Most best practices scholars follow John Dewey in viewing their contributions as different than mainstream "hands-off" social science and abstract academic theory-building: their action-orientation seeks to prove its worth over time through trial and error implementation.[5]

Seen from the standpoint of the hermeneutics of suspicion, however, best practices studies are methodologically and politically naïve. They fail to capture important patterns and flaws in democratic innovation over the past two decades. At a systemic level it is difficult to argue that American politics or civil society has become more reflective and partici-patory in any respect related to the rather small bore democratic innova-tion activity. Despite the growing numbers of innovative practices, such as citizen forums, the impact appears negligible. Practitioners have made only poorly defined linkages between their local innovations and the larger world of concrete decision-making—whether at the local, state, or national levels, in the different branches of government, and among other major so-cial institutions. What appear as "best practices" are typically freestanding experiments with little capacity to present advice to official bodies holding decision-making power, not to mention exercise any actual decision-making power of their own. Moreover, contrasted with the optimistic reports of how democratic innovations strengthen citizenship, there is evidence that they may also depress, constrain, and contort citizen agency in certain reg-ular, patterned ways.

Finding their bearings from the theoretical analysis of neoliberalism of scholars such as Wendy Brown and Colin Crouch, but empirically grounded in qualitative sociology, scholars such as Nina Eliasoph, Caroline Lee, Michael McQuarrie, and Edward Walker argue that democratic innovations such as citizen forums are simply no match for neoliberal forces of privatization and, indeed, in a number of important respects have been propelled forward by these forces.[6] Focusing on a wide range of practitioners of "civic engagement," "community service," and "deliberative democracy," they argue that academic advocates of participatory innovation and practitioners alike have been naïve about economic power, leaving so-called "best practices" to work to the advantage of elites. Community engagement efforts have helped legitimate the offloading of public sector responsibilities on to the private sector and to individual citizens who may not be able to afford to pick up the tab. When participatory public events go well, they reinforce norms of individual action to the detriment of potentially more radical social movement collective action. When they go poorly, they breed cynicism and pessimism, which are also demobilizing. Either way the elites win.

Pause to notice how the hermeneutics of suspicion differs from what I have called the commonplace or "realist" critique of participatory democracy, which stresses the *ineffectual* nature of democratic innovation. Instead of joining these critics in judging participatory practices as relatively harmless, if useless, freewheels spinning along without engaging the real world of politics, the hermeneutics of suspicion argues that such public engagement efforts *do* engage the real world of politics—by depressing opposition mobilization, by individuating political action, and by helping counter-democratic officials and private sector actors shapeshift into seemingly benign civic influences.

A major concern, therefore, is to be more cognizant of what might be fueling the demand for participatory innovations: Is it really coming from those with broad public interests at heart? Critics suspect that a significant part of the demand is generated by elites who favor neoliberalism in government and free market structures in the economy. Because of the social disruptions already occurring as a result of shifts in these directions, elites in and out of government require community engagement and public forums nurturing "authentic dialogue" to give the appearance of taking citizens' concerns seriously, but also to shift some of the responsibility for public welfare over to the public itself. Public forums proliferated in California, for example, between 2008 and 2009 to avoid conflict over "appropriation and distribution of public resources" and "smooth the process of fiscal bargaining, by allowing public officials to calibrate their fiscal demands more carefully to the political tolerance of the citizenry."[7] Participatory practices became entrenched in the civic life of Cleveland over the last generation not because they effectively translated community interests into public policy, but because they served as a kind of placebo, a proxy substitute for effective policy that helped legitimate officials even as urban decline became more and more evident.[8] In the private sector, "corporations, industry groups, and wealthy advocacy organizations regularly seek to mobilize participation in public life as a strategy to enhance their sociopolitical legitimacy, and a multi-million dollar industry has emerged to help facilitate public engagement on behalf of these interests."[9]

Though their focus may seem like crude "follow the money" economic determinism, hermeneutics of suspicion scholars are not arguing that elites are directly manipulating the form or content of these ostensibly public practices. Stakeholders actually want forums in which "real" community reflection and dialogue flourishes. They already buy one-way public relations communications, after all, through conventional advertisements in a range of media. What they are funding when they sponsor public forums is a kind of authenticity; the less these study circles and citizen round tables look like the patterns of strategic discourse common in political institutions and business firms, the more "civic" and "public spirited" the forum stakeholders writing the checks will appear. Further, public forum dialogue that is pragmatic and open-minded, non-ideological, resistant to being politicized toward social justice ends, and constructive not adversarial, is extremely useful for elites seeking acquiescence to the dramatic changes neoliberalism has already ushered in.[10] This process cannot appear as co-optation by elites, for that would undermine the objective of authenticity. This kind of discourse, nevertheless, produces numerous constraints on citizen agency.[11]

What elites purchase, critics argue, is a kind of "technology of participation" that in no uncertain terms is meant to give citizens voice, albeit without any resources or means attached for efficacious choice. Over the last two decades, even as participatory innovations have grown more common, public policies promoting social well-being and economic equality have receded as achievable objectives. "Participation is no longer a threat to elites; it is a resource" because forums "underpin the authority of urban elites when promises of growth are understood to be empty."[12] Of course, since what is being funded is non-ideological pragmatic discourse, stakeholders are safe to assume that pointed critiques of neoliberalism, corporate power, or economic inequality will not emerge from most nonpartisan public forums: "even if participants might prefer it: any critique of corporate power has a big roadblock in front of it."[13]

Indeed, elite stakeholders in participatory innovations can come to look like citizens, good neighbors, even while they are playing powerful shaping roles in the background of government institutions, in the market, and in the broader public world. This "flattening" of asymmetries of economic and political power can make it difficult for citizens to resist, confront, and meaningfully engage.[14] Another outcome closely related to flattening is fragmentation and dispersion. Democratic forums can sprout up anywhere—in a coffee shop, library, school, conference hotel—and can involve elected officials, celebrities, media figures, university faculty, and many others loosely or tightly involved in the world of governance. While practitioners advocate them as a refreshing alternative to constraining three-minutes-at-the-microphone public discourse common in mainstream formal political institutions, these forums are actually creating significant fragmentation and dispersion in the public sphere. Even if the least one can say is that it is difficult to tell a civic forum from a sham event entirely saturated by a neoliberal agenda, still that is a victory for neoliberalism because doubt has been seeded in the public culture about whether participatory forums are genuine platforms for developing public ideas and action plans.[15]

Rather than seeing democratic innovations through best practices lenses as efforts, some more effective than others, at public education and community empowerment—let a thousand flowers bloom!—hermeneutics of suspicion scholars frame them in terms of social control: public forums absorb potentially critical citizen agency and channel it in demotivating and individuating non-oppositional directions. Forums subtly demotivate participants by muting criticism of elites and by encouraging the acceptance of elite authority. The non-ideological pragmatic conversations facilitated in community round tables, often placing policy choices along a range of possibilities abstracted from social and economic conflicts, deflects challenges to institutional actors and, even more important, shapes the critique of elites in ways favorable to neoliberalism. Expressions of disillusionment with "formal political institutions" and "mainstream politics" common in such public forums are not, of course, tunes composed by neoliberal-friendly elites, but they are music to their ears and one reason for writing the checks. "Tropes critical of institutions dovetail neatly with neoliberal ideologies promoting expert private-sector management over ineffective, out-of-touch bureaucracies."[16] The critical discourse that does surface in forums—about profit-making at the expense of social goals, or bureaucratic inefficiency, or hierarchical calcification—is "old news" already incorporated into standard corporate business norms and neoliberal governance practice.[17] Officials organizing community meetups gain legitimacy by being seen to encourage as open an exchange of citizen views as possible, whether or not those views ever get translated into action.[18]

Another social control effect frequently produced in public forums, note critics, is the promotion of a certain kind of image of the good citizen: a person with self-reliance, economic discipline, thrift, and related business

virtues. Common in facilitated community forums on youth issues, for example, is the idea of "empowerment through self-discipline."[19] Or consider how participants in Cleveland's community-based organizations were
encouraged to reconceive their definition of "civic" to stress "ownership, participation, and individual responsibility, in opposition to dependence, tran-
sience, and tolerance" and ultimately to "measure neighborhood well-being"
in terms of real estate values.[20] Obviously, the celebration of business virtues
dovetails with neoliberal objectives, such as the offloading of responsibility
for social problems such as poverty, inadequate education or healthcare or
housing, even while the prospects for taking up such responsibility appear
daunting. "Events that emphasize constructive solution generation even in
dire circumstances," notes Caroline Lee, "may limit more substantive political action by providing opportunities for small-scale change and allowing
stakeholders to vent. Citizens are encouraged to govern themselves as a way
of enacting civic virtue: by eating responsibly and staying healthy, by caring
for their spouses and parents, and by making sure their children are educated,
productive members of society." Such community engagement is "cold com-
fort when those small-scale actions become back-breaking—when an under-
insured person becomes sick, when an aging breadwinner is laid off, or when
caring for a partner or parent with dementia interferes with her loved ones'
ability to contribute to that economy." While community round tables and
study circles encourage a "nonpartisan win-win spirit," their lack of purchase
on social problems can become "a cruel joke for some."[21]

Though appearing to re-engage citizens in the political life of their
communities, critics suspect that many individual self-help and small group
volunteer efforts deflect people away from the larger social justice efforts
or political movements that could challenge elite power. Volunteers do not
question the source of social problems such as poverty, they just pitch in to
attempt to directly help—often fairly ineffectually—those affected, say, by
serving as after-school counselors for marginalized youth. Activists, by contrast, see problems such as poverty as matters of justice and human decision-
making and therefore as conflicts; by "connecting the dots," they seek to move
issues from private to public and into the realm of politics.[22] Citizen engagement efforts that channel civic agency into volunteerism rather than activism
thus defuse the potential politicization of social issues and protect established
official and private sector interests in the status quo. When citizen forums go
well, they reinforce commitments to individual agency as opposed to collective action and generate support for event stakeholders as opposed to pro-
voking oppositional claims for social justice. When they fail, and participants

leave without absorbing much information or achieving deliberative clarity, they create cynicism and pessimism that are also demobilizing. "*The end result of all of these little steps to empowerment is, unfortunately, not a long journey to social justice,*" Lee argues, "*but a tightening spiral of resignation and retreat from public life to our increasingly demanding domestic worlds.*"[23]

Here hermeneutics of suspicion scholars join thinkers critical of democratic innovation from the perspective of deeply rooted social justice principles. For example, significant skepticism about the idea of democratizing criminal justice persists among scholars and activists who argue, from a social justice perspective, that under conditions of severe racial inequality any attempt at reform that does not seek racial justice as a primary and fundamental goal at the outset will fail, and among abolitionists claiming that punishment is always coercive, degrading, and therefore necessarily incompatible with true democracy.[24] For social justice critics, as with hermeneutics of suspicion scholars, participatory innovations are akin to palliative care: they may mute or cover over chronic problems, but they offer no cure, as the causes—social, racial, and economic conflicts—remain undiagnosed and unaddressed.

Strengths and Weaknesses of Critique

Hermeneutics of suspicion scholars alert reform-minded advocates to the ways some public engagement efforts may be unwittingly dampening citizen agency while smoothing over legitimate sources of social conflict, and they indicate some powerful political and economic forces subtly encouraging such tendencies. Nevertheless, even while offering bracingly critical accounts of participatory innovation, these scholars do not intend to be purely oppositional. Indeed, they aim to contribute to the democratic revitalization project shared with best practices scholars. Viewed in this light, the hermeneutics of suspicion is an attempt at identifying what innovations are vulnerable to co-optation and which professional attitudes and practices are problematic for democracy, so those working in this area can examine, evaluate, and endorse modes of civic action, collaboration, and co-production that could stand the test of time as "real" or "authentic" power-sharing resources. To get to this more constructive core, however, we have to pare away a few elements of the critique that are overstated and, in fact, may be corrosive to the goals of building a more participatory democracy.

First, the sober de-mythologizing of the active and reflective citizen celebrated and encouraged by democratic professionals is helpful in identifying the ways forums and other participatory innovations fail to support meaningful civic agency, but hermeneutics of suspicion scholars often paint an overly bleak picture for readers involved in democratic practices or seeking to become more engaged in their communities. At times, critique turns to a toxic skepticism of lay power-sharing akin to Max Weber's *Protestant Ethic* portrayal of the "iron cage of modernity" or Michel Foucault's claustrophobic account of near-invisible webs of "capillary" power formations creating but also trapping modern subjects. Naming public engagement practices *"technologies of participation* that would make participation safe for use as a component of the authority of elites," for example, alerts us to the ways some may be instrumental, top-down, and manipulative, but if taken as a blanket conceptualization, it forecloses on the possibility that some of these practices might actually be dialogical, collaborative, and empowering to non-elites in any meaningful fashion.[25] The assertion that democratic innovations can be co-opted slides into generalized mistrust of the participatory democratic project tout court, facilitators and citizens who have taken part in it, as well as core concepts such as "public." As Walker notes, "we can no longer simply equate participation with empowerment and shared governance; the very notion of the public has been transformed in such a fashion that participation is often a means of defending established practices by states and market actors."[26]

Doubt about the civic efficacy of laypeople involved in particular community projects or deliberative forums can cascade into a deeper pessimism regarding the political subjectivity of the groups being convened. The participation "industry" has caused a "shift in the constitution of the public," continues Walker; "the modern public has been redefined such that it becomes exceedingly difficult to distinguish between types of participation that have true empowering potential from those that reinforce institutionalized practices in state and market organizations."[27] Hermeneutics of suspicion scholars at times call into question not just the authenticity of collective action facilitated in a particular public forum, but the project of convening publics itself, or as Eliasoph puts it, the "vague constituency that they hope, in part to create," "this mythical constituency ... [they] call 'the public' ".[28] To be sure, intellectual skepticism regarding the idea of popular sovereignty grew up alongside the first eighteenth century practical formulations of it that fueled revolutionary rhetoric and constitutional principles alike; the idea will survive, but such doubt about the capacity of people to form and govern themselves is more disabling to the project of democratic renewal they endorse than the hermeneutics of suspicion scholars realize. No longer explanatory or descriptive, concepts such as "mythical constituency" and "participatory technologies" are warnings that promote generalized wariness about joining in these group efforts rather than encouraging a keen awareness of strengths and weaknesses of collective processes.

Second, because they incline toward traditional social justice activism pressing for greater state intervention and provision, hermeneutics of suspicion analyses can appear ahistorical and unaware of current constraints on political action. While correct in drawing out the limited purchase on social and institutional change available to some kinds of citizen engagement, these critics have an idealized image of social movements and collective protests in the background of their political reflections.

> When the balance goes out of whack between civic, state, and market forces, civic organizations keep popping up to reset it, but these associations are not placid do-gooders who feed the homeless without asking why there is homelessness. They are rebels. In the USA, Greece, Iceland, Spain, Canada, and elsewhere, some grassroots activists are rebelling against the idea that the market can solve everything, and are starting to become political activists, when they "connect the dots."[29]

No doubt, social movements, grassroots activists, and rebels help "connect the dots," but they are not the only or even, in some cases, the best, ways of achieving democratic renewal. Indeed, as we noted earlier in the Preface, some of the most significant flaws of contemporary democratic innovation, such as proliferation, fragmentation, and the individuating of lay citizen agency, have also been found in nationally organized social movement structures that leave communities on the sidelines, even while working strenuously for specific, albeit narrow, public interests.[30] Further, hermeneutics of suspicion scholars seem to have a fairly traditional view of social activism as speaking hard truths to centralized forms of economic and social power and pressuring federal officials and major corporate elites to change their ways.[31]

The protest, or social movement, form of democratic agency is without question necessary and important. When seen as the only or the best mode of efficacious collective action, however, it can severely limit the prospect for renewal because it mistakenly treats as trivial more small-bore and local citizen politics. As I have argued throughout this book, drawing on the work of Harry Boyte, Henrik Bang, Peter Levine, and others, citizen agency in the form of "public work" and "everyday making" and "co-production" is not a distraction from activist politics of social movements, and it is not in any kind of zero-sum contest with it.[32] The kinds of participatory democratic innovation I endorse are efforts at sharing power and responsibility that go beyond asking elites to make better law or policy or rulings *for us*; they ask elites to work *with us*. This kind of everyday civic agency, which differs from the advocacy work of social movement activists, on the one hand, and apolitical volunteerism on the other, is largely neglected by the hermeneutics of suspicion.

Another place where the hermeneutics of suspicion is too wide-ranging in its critique has to do with skepticism about forum proliferation. If the concern is that citizen forums, neighborhood study circles, and civic round tables do little more than talk, that worry is warranted only if the talk is non-deliberative, uninformative, or is a distraction from more formal decision-making. But these claims have not been proven; at most, hermeneutics of suspicion has shown how some citizens' forums have failed to successfully link to substantive decision-making.[33] While pop-up, short-term, low-impact forums can indicate superficiality, to be sure, they can also in some contexts signal widespread citizen interest in public issues. Further, proliferation and diversity of novel forms of engagement can be a healthy sign of an elite willingness to share power rather than a dysfunctional and manipulative distraction undermining citizen efficacy. Recall the example of Decatur, Georgia, where public administrators took pains to proliferate public forums not to distract, but to organize community efforts in as widespread a fashion as possible; their goal was to experiment so frequently, and to add so many different forms for people to get involved, that a self-sustaining civic environment would emerge and persist into the future. The essential question is whether proliferation of diverse forms of collective talk and action is helping people get better organized, networked, and connected to meaningful social or political work inside and outside institutions.

An Agenda for Democratic Inquiry and Evaluation

We can use what appears sound in the hermeneutics of suspicion to develop a critical but also constructive framework for evaluating democratic innovation. Looking for functional connections between democratic innovations and active citizens and keeping alert to counter-democratic patterns, I see four lines of inquiry that could help cultures of participatory democratic innovation grow and become more meaningful for the people involved.

A high priority is to discover strategies to block or dilute the privatization of public engagement, as this appears most corrosive to real ground-level citizen problem-solving. Transparency about funding sources draws a bright line between, for example, free-flowing discourse and more tailored forums with potential strings attached. As we have seen with participatory innovation in education, criminal justice, and public administration, public engagement does not require corporate funding; while no doubt resource intensive in terms of volunteer and participant time, most other costs are negligible. Critical sensitivity—though not pessimism—should also be brought to bear on public sector deliberation to call out instrumental forms of citizen engagement intended to pacify, distract, or manufacture symbolic legitimacy for administrative decisions already made in advance. That sensitivity is useful as well for identifying non-manipulative power-sharing forms of citizen-oriented professionalism within public administration, for example. Indeed, there is much to learn at the ground level about what kinds of collective projects, deliberative forums, and public work efforts are experienced as "owned" by citizens and communities themselves. Longevity, increased rates of participation, and levels of personal identification with group goals, among other indicators, may be measurable proxies of this kind of public "ownership."

A second major objective is shoring up the democratic professionalism of innovators so they can push back against social, political, and economic pressures threatening the efficacy of collective action. This means reinforcing professional norms that empower laypeople, as Eliasoph notes, writing about the kinds of democratic social workers Jane Addams trained: "part of what expertise might mean is knowledge about how to get ordinary people involved in decision-making in ways that genuinely will help them." "Professionals, especially professional social workers, may have enough experience, and enough of the big picture, to 'connect the dots.' "[34] Shoring up democratic professionalism also means encouraging deep reflection about the meaning of expertise, knowledge, and skill in the context of social problem-solving. Beyond working with citizens as partners in a shared process of "connecting the dots," democratic professionals think of problem-solving capabilities as multifaceted, and co-created, and therefore not "owned" by a specific agent or group. They understand social problems such as homelessness, school-to-prison pipelines, domestic violence, and lack of fair and fulfilling work not as the expert domains of the well-trained but as requiring long term collaborative partnerships between reform-minded professional practitioners in schools, police departments, prisons, community hospitals; members of community organizations; participants in activist networks; as well as interested and uninterested citizens alike.

A third major aim is to avoid the demobilizing and individuating tendencies of some forms of civic engagement practices. Scholars have suggested practical ways of closing gaps between activism and nonpartisan public engagement. Polletta points out that "guaranteeing 'meaningful' forums may require that the sponsoring organization move from serving as 'broker' to serving as public advocate for the positions arrived at in the forum."[35] For example, the inefficacious post-9/11 "Listening to the City" citizen forums taking up the question of what to build at Ground Zero could have done more to combine reflective discussion with advocacy: "What if organizers had repeatedly reminded authorities that 'the people' wanted not only an iconic tower but also affordable housing at the site; not only the restoration of the street grid but also a reduction of the amount of planned office space? Might things have turned out differently?"[36] Demobilizing and individuating tendencies may exist, but they are not "baked in" to public engagement efforts per se. "Listening to the City" failed to "connect the dots," but could have if it had been structured differently. While difficult, switching to advocacy or community organizing work after a mostly conversational process is possible and can be valuable for activists and non-activists alike.

Finally, and perhaps most essential, is to determine how well citizen engagement efforts are connected to, and relevant for, actual social problem-solving in the sometimes repellent institutional world. Building on the grounded democratic theory of Rosanvallon and others, throughout this book citizen participation has been conceptualized to stress actual institutional power-sharing, in forms such as monitoring and evaluating norms and policy, taking part in co-creating the "product" of institutions—whether it is "education," "justice," or "governance"—and rendering public judgments, among other modes.[37] Even in the most repellent institutional domain of criminal justice, which blocks lay citizen outsiders from some aspects of monitoring, evaluating, co-creating, and judging, we have seen that other aspects of exactly these kinds of power-sharing are possible for citizens to take up, if democratic professionals working in and alongside these institutions help open the doors: to citizen review boards that monitor and evaluate and advise police and prosecutors; to jurors serving in trial courts, to citizens volunteering in restorative justice programs, to students and faculty building educational rehabilitative connections to inmates. These are different than traditional social movement efforts but hold no less value for creating a better democracy; citizens may not be pressing on elites in formal institutions to do something, but they are, themselves, doing public work that aims to carry out the social problem-solving functions of an institutional world re-centered and re-anchored in the public domain.

Keeping hermeneutics of suspicion warnings about elite pressures and demotivating individuation at the forefront of our awareness, we can also notice the wide range of citizen-staffed public work already happening routinely all around us. This work is best evaluated as horizontally as possible, not triumphed as a potential TED talk on "life hacks for democracy" or dismissed as a doomed twist of the Dialectic of Enlightenment, but as something in which writers, thinkers, and researchers also have a stake. Just as with practitioners in other fields, there are barriers and openings to democratic professionalism in academia, which we will note in the next and final chapter, and a fundamental step is to think of inquiry as a collective project bridging action, reflection, experience, and discussion in an ongoing reform effort.

Democratic Professionalism, Activism, and Democratic Inquiry in Unexpected Places

Democratic professionalism, activism, and democratic inquiry can fruitfully coalesce. Few torchbearers of participatory democracy would imagine flickering embers being fanned in mental healthcare. Yet there is increasing interest in the United Kingdom in the counterintuitive prospect of democratic facilities. Mental health professionals, current and former service users, activists, and academics are working together to seek major changes in this field. While still in its early stages, this network is making inroads via professional training, collaborative institutional evaluation studies, and highly inclusive nongovernmental organizations forging practical relationships with clinics and other mental health institutions. This case is instructive in the ways participatory innovation is being evaluated as an ongoing part of a horizontal collaboration, and it suggests how calls for democratization within institutions can link together disparate groups in pressing for more power-sharing.

Democracy and Co-production

Advocates talk about "democratizing" the mental health profession to draw attention to something missing in ongoing debates about how to improve mental healthcare and, more specifically, to provide more robust institutional scaffolding for ideas of shared decision-making circulating among reformers since the 1980s. "In my view," argues Mick McKeown, an academic and mental health nursing practitioner, "mental health professionalism certainly needs re-thinking and re-organizing and the prospect of addressing the pivotal issue of power in the social relations of care appears to be central to any critical consideration of co-production."[38] Co-production rejects therapeutic attitudes, habits, and language that place people in need of treatment in positions of passivity, holding that even people in severe mental distress possess resources that can contribute to overcoming their difficulties. One-directional, top-down therapeutic relationships routinely fail to identify these resources, can dampen down individual agency, and foster dependency. Advocates of co-production use the phrase "healing together" to register the ways mental health recovery is a social not an individual effort, with family members, neighbors, co-workers, and former patients all serving as a fundamental, not merely ancillary, support system. Co-production signals a change in how mental health professionalism is understood, away from a technocratic model centered on medical expertise in which the practitioner is a storehouse of knowledge and a set of therapeutic skills. Advocates urge a multifaceted and humanistic account of mental health professionals as human beings who learn from the people they help and who themselves thrive via mutual not self-enclosed relationships.

Reformers such as McKeown use the term "democracy" concretely, not symbolically, to critique power imbalances and to insist on the inclusion of marginalized people in decisions affecting them. They challenge normalized hierarchical relations between mental health professionals and patients, draw attention to the ways power and authority are typically justified, and seek out other modes of legitimation. University training, credentialing, expertise, and legal authority to prescribe all serve to legitimate professional power, yet they can obstruct the development of horizontal relationships conducive for "healing together." Reformers also criticize the tendency of mental health facilities to strip people of dignity in sealed-off spaces, where patients and their family members are relatively powerless second-class citizens. For them, "democracy" means a set of particular norms and practices allowing patients and family members to have a voice, a seat at the table, a measure of respect and influence in guiding and managing treatment plans.

Stressing "democracy" helps bolster professionals' commitments to co-production, which can be readily absorbed into established technocratic patterns of mainstream institutions and co-opted as just another set of boxes to check. "Democracy" identifies a significant gap in current practice while aligning reforms with an alternative conception of legitimate power and authority. "Co-production," notes Pamela Fisher, a sociologist active in the democratizing mental health network, "involves genuine power-sharing and therefore a fundamental democratizing of relationships between professionals and service users in mental health. Understood this way, co-production is more radical than shared decision-making which can leave power imbalances intact."[39]

Reflecting on the history of mental health reform, Sarah Carr, an academic and activist, argues that emancipatory ideas have frequently turned repressive in the absence of actual power-sharing inside. Rules and roles shaped in the highly coercive era of asylums are still found in today's ostensibly liberal and progressive institutions. "There is a lot of groundwork that needs to be done to ensure that co-production can occur properly. And that means exploring and addressing some of the age old power dynamics that go on between practitioners and between service users."[40] Democratizing mental health, in Carr's view, involves reform-minded professionals who do more than band together to improve institutions; they must forge continued connections to outside activism and allow it to come inside. "There needs to be room for disruption," Carr argues, "and safe spaces for people to explore how angry they are," meaning both staff and service users.[41] Progressive liberal commitments to openness and transparency are still important institutional values, but the democratization movement presses for more: the actual circulation of activists, especially former mental health patients, into the institutional life of clinics. Current and former patients have useful lay knowledge about what works in the recovery process, what is lacking in particular institutions, and what specific resources are needed to forge healthy therapeutic relationships.

Democratic Professionalism, Participatory Innovation, and Democratic Inquiry

One measure underway by reformers is the resocialization of professionals via early career university training. This involves critically questioning traditional models of professionalism and discussing how power-sharing can be integrated into routine practice. As Fisher puts this, "co-production is not the same as patient and public involvement, it is about power sharing, and power sharing requires new approaches to professionalism."[42] Quite a lot of "unlearning" has to happen to encourage practitioners to replace token involvement of service users with power-sharing in the fast-paced and uncertain environments of mental healthcare clinics. University and public sector events for mid-career professionals include choice-work exercises conducted with patients to sensitize people to the decision-making abilities of service users. More difficult, but a central focus of reform advocacy nevertheless, are planned changes to ward rounds and other mental health inpatient settings. Because of the historical weakness of ethics codes and the insufficiency of professional standards, reformers are pressing for power-sharing and for continued leverage to ensure horizontal relationships. "Addressing imbalances of power goes to the core of co-production" says Fisher, "and space—in different forms—seems important for resisting power." Though conceptually amorphous, "space" means something quite concrete and specific to democratic reformers such as Fisher: designated areas or scheduled times to question, to dissent, and to offer contrasting opinions—"space to talk, to feel safe, to think, to innovate, to do things differently, to help blur roles and demarcations."[43]

Embedded in democratization reforms are new ways of involving current and former service-users to examine institutional practice in mental health facilities, shape questions and plan out how to conduct research, set standards for evaluation, and draw up future targets for organizational transformation. Academics Gemma Stacey and Philip Houghton, working in the Critical Values Based Practice Network of mental health reformers, collaborated with patients on a study that revealed the routinely incomplete and sporadic nature of the treatment information communicated by busy professionals with patients and their families. In response, this research team offered a practical three "i" approach to correct the problem, through which patients would be more regularly "informed," "involved," and "influential." The "ideal ward round," note Stacey and Houghton, "is underpinned by an alternative model of decision making which recognises the constraints of this practice setting and encourages decisions to be viewed as on a continuum whereby shared influence over the outcome of decisions is the gold standard but information about the decision making process is a minimum expectation."[44] Another collaborative research team, the Bristol Co-production Group, led by a service-user, a mental health professional, and an academic, has developed co-production educational materials for mental health nursing students.

A chronic issue in mental health reform is how to enact, support, and sustain ideal ward rounds and innovative co-productive norms when only some staff members are motivated. How can the democracy-minded organize to support innovation and engage those more comfortable with the status quo at their facilities? Nongovernmental voluntary organizations can help serve as quasi-institutional resources for ongoing patient support and advocacy inside and alongside mental health facilities, especially when these organizations include service-users. Former patient Tina Coldham illustrates this approach with her Social Care Institute for Excellence, which aims to "co-produce our work with people who use services and their carers to identify what works and how that knowledge can be put into practice." "We have a co-production charter," she says, "to help guide our work. We conducted a board recruitment recently and out of four new members three identify as disabled people."[45] Routine integration of formerly marginalized laypeople into a resistant professional domain aims to gradually influence those staff members currently entrenched in mainstream models of hierarchical therapeutic relationships.

Inclusionary Network Building

How can there be any kind of real "democracy" in mental health when asymmetry and inequality seem an inextricable part of therapy? The doctor hasn't sought treatment from the patient, after all, and the patient may not be capable of making good decisions. This pointed question helps reveal an easily made misconception regarding the targets of these reforms: democratization of mental health is not de-professionalization and it is not anti-expertise—it is about making changes in the organization of mental health institutions to allow greater power-sharing and more genuine dialogue. A patient with a condition such as severe schizophrenia would have difficulty taking up a significant role in co-producing a treatment plan; nevertheless, his or her parent, or partner, or friend, or long-time neighbor might be able and very willing to do so. The fundamental issue has to do with how, when, and where to implement these participatory democratic norms. Regardless of the particular condition, recovering patients, former patients, family members, and advocates all can play more significant roles than they are currently allowed. A severely incapacitating condition experienced by a patient is no bar to extending the inclusionary organizing principles of democratic reformers to her support networks; they are useful, too, for helping the patient herself move forward through the clinic and in the social world outside.

A patient may be at a low point at the moment of seeking treatment, yet also have skills and accomplishments in the outside world that can be an useful part of a treatment plan if mental health professionals were attuned and open to dialogue. A service-user has assets not just deficits, but these have to be perceived, valued, and integrated into decision-making. The local knowledge of the patient and family caregivers can be critically important and yet is often dismissed or downgraded. The label "expert by experience" has been used to assert institutional status by family caregivers seeking open and respectful dialogue and more authority inside mental health facilities to better manage the transition back outside.

Democratic professional reforms resonate with clinic staff seeking meaningful work in more horizontal organizations; while challenging to the status quo, they are not anti-professional or dismissive of the value of institutions. They have also appealed to networks of outside reformers who recognize the limits of earlier liberal and progressive reforms— transparency, patient autonomy, ethics codes—that leave professional power and hierarchy intact. For deeper and more durable reform, advocacy by and on behalf of mental health service-users must be a persistent and circulatory force, finding ways to integrate into the routine work done at clinics and wards. Yet advocates see professionals as potential allies not obstacles to reconstruction. In a way that may be instructive for the professional domains we have focused on in this book, we see activists' advocacy work and external critique constructively interact with routine institutional functioning. There is surprising grass-roots optimism among reformers in this movement: fully aware of the history of the asylum, they reject the assumption that mental health professionals will inevitably reproduce Goffman-like "total institutions" hidden away from society. Along with bringing the robust participatory norms expected on the "outside" into clinics and wards, democratizers are also working to bring people on the "inside" into the pathways, public spaces, and regular activities of the neurotypical social world.

As the hermeneutics of suspicion makes clear, it is important to remain critically attentive to ways ostensibly "democratic" relationships might disguise further concentrations of power. Vigilance about the authenticity of co-production must be constant in all domains in which these new standards of practice are put forward. "Ultimately," notes Pamela Fisher, "co-production can be evidenced by the extent to which professionals change their minds and practices—and the extent to which services are shaped by the people using them."[46] Close attention must be paid to how well reforms are in fact sustained and expanded in institutions with no small traces left of the asylum. Yet this highly critical yet also constructive network offers important lessons in how democratic professional reforms, participatory innovation, and horizontal inquiry can work together to empower marginalized people.

Conclusion

Now I will do nothing but listen,
To accrue what I hear into this song, to let sounds
contribute toward it.

—WALT WHITMAN

Seedbeds

How can critical and constructive reform networks emerge? If one is out-side a professional field or institution, is there anything one can contribute to support the development of democratic collaboration and power-sharing in-side? There is no simple answer, but three things may be helpful in cultivating democratic professionalism. First, existing *networks* of democracy-minded professionals in education, criminal justice, and public administration need to be shored up. There is significant fragmentation at the moment and hardly any cross-fertilization between different fields. In some areas, such as public ad-ministration, there is much interest in public engagement among mainstream professional organizations. In others, such as K-12 education and criminal jus-tice, there is considerably more wariness, at least in established groups. There is a role to be played here by nonprofit organizations concerned with citizen agency and democratic renewal to facilitate cross-disciplinary meetings and workshops so that innovators can gather, share notes, and get ideas.

Second, specific *paths* and *signposts* developed in one place may be useful elsewhere, especially if widely known. One purpose of this project has been to draw out particularly compelling stories of people who have created real spaces of democratic agency, to show how it can be done, to point out the hurdles involved but also the available resources. School districts vary and po-litical cultures shift at the state border, but democratic principals and teachers can help illustrate administrative and pedagogical practices that apply across many different environments: the all school meeting, the school constitution, the peer jury or conflict resolution process. The same is true of democratic professionals in public administration and criminal justice who demonstrate how participatory innovations can take shape under difficult circumstances. While wary of best practices and role models, I think more stories about democratic professionals' experiences can spark awareness of institutions as real, malleable, and subject to reclamation rather than looming, abstract and bloodless, in the distance.

A third possible seedbed of democratic professionalism is *higher education*. Colleges and universities are gatekeepers to the professional world, where access requires increasingly specialized degrees and advanced training. Catalysts of normative orientation, college programs can be places where young people can articulate their concerns about the world they are entering, gain skills, and develop tools for change. Yet, with a few exceptions, the democratic professionals I have interviewed are emerging despite university training not because of it. Rather than serving as sites of possible leverage to help professions transition to a more democratic model, universities are often marked by the same repellent, technocratic, and self-serving tendencies we have seen operative in other professional fields as barriers to more participatory norms.

People in Glass Houses

I became aware of the problem even before I started my research on innovative democratic professionals. For years I have included on some of my syllabi the "Port Huron Statement" written by Tom Hayden and others in the Students for a Democratic Society. As we have noted, Hayden advocates cooperative workplaces, open social relations, and citizen-oriented governing institutions. He urges his fellow students to recognize and make use of their universities as sites of transformative change: as models of participatory democracy and channels for transmitting these values into the outside world. Committed to collegiality and truth seeking, faculty listen to good reasons, and their seminars are places of critical dialogue in which students can challenge repressive, hierarchical, and self-interested practices on campus and in society at large, thus sensitizing and activating their fellows in close proximity in classrooms and campus gathering places. As graduates take their places in corporate and public worlds, they will incrementally remake the institutions therein in a more participatory democratic fashion.

Hayden's narrative pictures the university as more egalitarian and invested in cultural change than it sometimes appears; underneath the tweeds, the ivy, and the scholasticism is a commitment to unconventional and disruptive ideas that clear new paths in math, science, and the humanities. Yet students reading "Port Huron" in my seminars tend to be unmoved. They care about reforming institutions and are far from apathetic, but the trouble is that students recognize their university is less democratic than it seems on the surface and is therefore an unsteady platform for transformative change. Academic creativity seems insular, self-referential, and beneficial to elites on and off campus. Universities only appear to be collegial, yet in reality often have closed off and hierarchical management structures. Relying on private search firms, trustees choose presidents and provosts with scant authentic input from below; once ensconced, these top administrators are typically evaluated with relatively non-transparent and non-participatory procedures. Administrative professionalism tends to follow a full-fledged social trustee model, with faculty, student, and community opinion rarely consulted with any seriousness. The absence of a vibrant democratic professionalism is evident, too, in the classroom and in daily faculty–student non-interaction. Though research and disciplinary specialization are commonly blamed for these academic tendencies, the deeper problem is a proximity deficit: faculty members' inability to see and act with students as fellow citizens, as collaborators—if only neophytes—in a common public project of understanding and improving shared social, political, and economic structures.

To be better seedbeds of participatory democracy, universities must convey through their own practices that institutions are not impervious to change, but are composed of real people with discernment, agency, fallibility, and a willingness to work across disciplinary, managerial, and generational divisions. Core ingredients of a more democratic academic culture include a commitment to power-sharing that in turn requires free speech, collegial respect, reciprocity, absence of unnecessary hierarchy, suspicion of lockstep proceduralism, and commitment to collective decision-making. Though many American colleges and universities systemically fail to live up to these norms, which are overpowered by the institutional forces we have been talking about—bureaucracy, routinization, legal accountability, risk management, and market definitions of efficiency and productivity—there is no small number of students, faculty, and administrators seeking openings to a more participatory culture.

Administrators who take up the challenge to become democratic professionals have a significant role to play in fostering dialogue with faculty and student committees with real responsibilities. For their part, faculty who accept the challenge can do much more to recognize students as co-creators of their education. Beyond receptivity to student voice and influence in seminars and in the shaping of curricula, there is the fundamental issue of how little time there is for research, student interaction, campus obligations, and work with community organizations. There is never enough time. To better cultivate norms of democratic practice, stakeholders need to find the time—fewer students per class, fewer classes per faculty member, fewer credits necessary to graduate—through some kind of calculus that respects research, students; and community.

Dangerous Outposts of a Humane Civilization?

Along with being more self-aware about their internal counter-democratic tendencies, to be contributors rather than barriers to an emerging culture of participatory innovation, colleges and universities need to look more carefully into the ways they think about instruction in professional and skilled work. Are they fostering—through their conceptual models, disciplinary knowledge, and training programs—widespread citizen agency and democratic self-determination, or are they mostly cultivating their own? Without a doubt, campus "civic engagement" programs and offices are thriving, but they are often freewheels spinning alongside the university's driving imperatives, which remain squarely attached to the social trustee model of managerial, technocratic professionalism.

Some of the very basic professional education choices to be made include, with specific reference to the fields we have focused upon in this book:

- criminal justice professionals can be taught to represent clients, deliver justice, and provide security to a largely passive populace or they can be taught to include citizens and neighborhoods in co-creating a just social order;
- public administrators can be prompted to devise cheaper and faster means of serving citizens as clients or they can be encouraged to involve citizens as equals in the planning process and in collaborative governance;
- schools of education can continue to pass along tried and true curricula fitting for largely passive classrooms or they can help teachers encounter students as people with voice and agency in co-producing their education.

The social trustee status quo will persist by default as long as higher education professionals complacently fail to recognize the costs of business as usual, which are paid out in the counter-democratic trends in contemporary institutions and concomitant levels of civic lethargy and public distrust. Students have a powerful role here, too, to question the professional fields many will enter upon leaving the university: What skills am I acquiring that can help me succeed not only in terms of status and financial reward, but in working with future colleagues to do better than our predecessors in humanizing our public institutions?

There are openings for critically minded and constructive students to press these issues on campus, to be sure, and there exist receptive professionals across disciplines in a wide variety of public, private, research, liberal arts, and specialized academic institutions.[1] Yet it is an uphill struggle for students and faculty alike. Many appear to be aware of the costs of the status quo, realizing the world the previous generations helped shape is one populated by providers and clients, producers and consumers, a world with profoundly undemocratic institutions that every day assert without even having to say it: "Lay citizens cannot do justice and cannot do public safety because we, the professionals, do that work for you." Internal problems plague mainstream professionalism, too, for institutions that treat people primarily as clients and consumers rather than active agents and partners do not adequately deliver goods such as justice and public safety, and are unfulfilling to work in because they separate professionals from important social sources of emotional nourishment and practical local knowledge.

The democratic professionals I have met reject institutional hypocrisy: the school that says it is educating citizens while providing no opportunities for self-government, or the prison that is so closed off to the public world that it cannot provide an avenue back into society for norm-violators. Undergraduates, graduate students, and faculty working in the natural and social sciences, arts and humanities, law, education, medicine, and engineering struggle with a similar situation. What many of us find desirable about our academic work—the freedom to choose intellectual projects; the collaborative aspect of research; the power-sharing in a laboratory, institute, or department; and the horizontal learning as new cohorts circulate through campus—is just what is being squeezed out of the misaligned and counter-democratic institutional domains we are unthinkingly supporting through our campuses' professional education and credentialing processes. We who administrate, teach, and study in professional education programs need to ask harder questions about what it means to be a professional today, and we need to seek some outside advice. Academics talk about the need for "public outreach" to spread ideas and best practices from the university out into the community; what I have in mind is the opposite. We need some "in-reach."

My suggestion here is humility. Academics are no vanguard, either in modeling democratic norms or offering theoretical models. We need to listen more, to take up the knowledge of people outside our normal disciplinary channels, to learn about the different modes of task-sharing, collaboration, co-ownership, and democratic divisions of labor that non-academic innovators are manifesting in daily life. We can help them form networks to share information and build platforms for problem-solving. By listening and learning, we can also incorporate some of their lessons of new democratic practice into higher education, striving toward the "dangerous outposts of a humane civilization" that Dewey hoped schools could become.[2]

A good example of this sort of recursiveness for higher education is a class on school redesign that democratic professional K-12 educator Helen Beattie recently taught at a Vermont college.

> Four schools are involved in this course. Each school has adults and students, teams of two to four from each school. The adults earn six graduate credits and the students are awarded college credit for a year-long class. We think we can't talk effectively about school redesign without the two primary stakeholders at the table.
>
> We are doing an action research design. This class is also going to be creating tools that will help guide students in fostering transformative dialogues. It will be a common language because the students are not going to let tools be developed that do not feel comfortable for them, and when it is comfortable for them it is comfortable for every stakeholder. There is nobody more masterful than students in getting to the heart of things. They play an essential role in co-creating what will serve their schools well as new strategies and techniques begin to take shape in response to state policy. These strategies are going to be steeped with youth-adult partnership.[3]

Beattie's class shows how academia can be a platform for horizontal collaboration with democratic professionals: not *training, instructing,* or *guiding* them, but *learning from* them, and even, in the best circumstances, *co-producing* with them. University *in-reach* allows reform-minded practitioners inside seminars and workshops to foster new thinking about professional skills.

Beyond Legislators and Interpreters: Doing Democratic Theory With and For

Focusing on the small territory of academia I work in called democratic theory, I want to conclude with some reflections on how we too might do the kind of "in-reach" that could better relate to innovators. This is harder than it might seem. Writing and thinking are such solitary activities—democracy is not. Worse, time spent writing and thinking is surely time not spent in an elected office making decisions, or in a neighborhood organizing a collective effort, or in a public space articulating grievances. Democratic theory, therefore, is always gnawing away against itself to some extent; in only the barest, most abstract sense does it seek others outside the world of thinking and writing. And this may explain why the others outside are not seeking us much, either.

One of the most sobering insights gained indirectly through my research is how distant democratic theory is from the work of people who are good at doing democracy. They become as smart as they are about democracy by doing it, by reflecting on it with others, but—this is the sobering part—never by dwelling on the texts I cherish in the academic canon. Democratic professionals do their work without help from any theory that resembles what we academics write. Names instantly recognizable to political theorists draw blank looks. This suggests completely different fields of thought and action rather than one shared field that has only to overcome a barrier between theory and practice.

To face this problem squarely, I think, is to practice democratic theory as a catalytic rather than traditionally academic discipline—meaning that research is done with and for the people being studied. *With* means listening carefully to democratic innovators, correcting and adjusting conceptual frameworks as one goes along, and taking suggestions on other lines of inquiry. *For* means contributing somehow to the success of their work by broadcasting it, encouraging discussion, and making links across professional domains to grow and diversify networks. Such an unabashedly open-ended and reform-minded methodological stance is not the only way to do democratic theory, of course, but it seems an appropriate expression of academic democratic professionalism: an admission of intellectual fallibility, sensitivity to the power of naming, humility in constructing theoretical frameworks, a commitment to task-sharing in concept building, and solidarity with those engaged in the never-ending project of humanizing the institutional world we shape and are shaped by.

Zygmunt Bauman classified modern intellectuals into two categories: "legislators" and "interpreters."[4] The former is a rational planner who seeks to influence law, policy, and culture to shape productive and fulfilling lives and relationships. The latter—aware on the one hand of the failures of rational social planning, yet appreciative of the wild diversity of productive and fulfilling lives—eschews the planning and shaping role and takes up the task of learning about other ways of life, and then translates these so that people might understand one another better. As Bauman himself realized, neither type of intellectual seems to matter in contemporary life, though they still offer their services in abundance in op-ed essays, think tank reports, and TED talks. The institutions are humming along without the goods proffered by intellectuals, and the people purportedly in need of shaping or interpreting are not paying much attention, either.

Legislators and interpreters are both "meta-professionals," people specializing in reason and careful methods who are somehow above and beyond practitioners as well as those others who are merely living their lives. To blaze a democratic professional rather than meta-professional path, however, I propose a third possibility: "active listeners." Active listeners do not build systems, yet we also do not just translate fixed meanings from one group to another; we are coequal—or try to be—in meaning making and system building. We open our ears, our eyes, our hearts, our minds, and we try to hear and see and feel and think more acutely, and, in our institution-shaping work and dialogue with others, we hold them to those expectations as well. We care about democracy, and we are troubled by the sneaky ways our own habits, norms, practices, and social structures on and off campus block and disable it.

I do not yet know how to make adequate use of active listening, or what narrative forms are the best vehicles for it, but it is evident that some of the most practically useful and theoretically rich texts in democratic theory are fascinating hybrids written by active listeners—from Montesquieu's *Spirit of the Laws* to Tocqueville's *Democracy in America* to Dewey's *Democracy and Education* and Mansbridge's *Beyond Adversary Democracy*. And pressures to reconnect to social problems at the ground level have produced significant recent methodological fermentation leading to more horizontal, inclusive, and action-oriented research programs among a number of contemporary disciplines.[5]

We will notice more of the world of actual and potential democracy, I think, and understand more about what we might contribute to it, if we assume that knowledge is created together, that concepts and theories move forward in conjunction with ground-level awareness earned through qualitative and participatory action research. As readers, too, we should ask if there is room in a theory for us, for our experiences, abilities, ideas, fears, and hopes. Democratic theory should not legislate for us, or merely interpret what we already know, but rather, invite us into the common project. Even in our anxious times, there is a world of democratic possibility to actively hear as we rebuild our public world—together.

Notes

PREFACE

1. David Mathews puts this point well when he writes about "a politics where citizens don't just comply or advise; they act. They get things done. They produce." *The Ecology of Democracy* (Kettering Foundation Press, 2014), p. 28.

2. According to the Pew Research Center, "Only 20% of Americans today say they can trust the government to do what is right 'just about always' (4%) or 'most of the time' (16%)." "Public Trust in Government Remains Near Historic Lows as Partisan Attitudes Shift," Pew Research Center Report (May 3, 2017). On declining trust among other advanced democracies, see Russell J. Dalton, "The Social Transformation of Trust in Government," *International Review of Sociology* 15 (2005) (1): 133–154.

3. See Theda Skocpol, *Diminished Democracy: From Membership to Management in American Civic Life* (Norman: University of Oklahoma Press, 2003).

4. To put this in perspective, consider Judge Jesse M. Furman, who has presided over only one criminal jury trial in the last four years at Manhattan's Federal District Court. "Trials are way, way down," reported his colleague, Judge Shira A. Scheindlin, "The building's quite dead." Benjamin Weiser, "Trial by Jury, a Hallowed American Right, Is Vanishing," *New York Times* (August 7, 2016). For countrywide decline, see Marc Galanter, "The Vanishing Trial: An Examination of Trials and Related Matters in Federal and State Courts," *Journal of Empirical Legal Studies* 1 (2004): 459–570.

5. Deborah Meier, "Democracy at Risk," *Educational Leadership* 66 (8) (2009): 46. The number of school boards is decreasing even while the population increases; Meier also notes how most are under the influence of mayors and city managers.

6. For a brief description of how meetings in a box were used recently to facilitate citizen discussion of city budget planning in Tallahassee, Florida, see Michelle Bono, "Tallahassee: A 2015 All American City," *National Civic Review* (Winter 2015): 41.

7. For a discussion of "stigmergy" that extends the concept from its original use in describing cooperative ant and termite behavior to broader application in human social organization, see Robert Moor, *On Trails* (New York: Simon and Schuster, 2016), pp. 72; 84–86.

CHAPTER 1

1. See Steven Brint, *In an Age of Experts: The Changing Role of Professionals in Politics and Public Life* (Princeton, NJ: Princeton University Press, 1994).
2. Talcott Parsons, "Professions," in *International Encyclopedia of the Social Sciences*, vol. 12 (New York: Macmillan, 1968), p. 536.
3. See, e.g., Ivan Illich, *Medical Nemesis: The Expropriation of Health* (New York: Random House, 1976); Michel Foucault, "Truth and Juridical Forms," in *Essential Works of Foucault, 1954–1984*, vol. 3, ed. P. Rabinow and J. D. Faubion (New York: The New Press, 2000), pp. 1–89
4. For more on these three types, see Albert W. Dzur, *Democratic Professionalism: Citizen Participation and the Reconstruction of Professional Ethics, Identity, and Practice* (University Park: Penn State University Press, 2008).
5. Sheldon S. Wolin, "Fugitive Democracy," *Constellations* 1 (1994): 11–25.
6. See Harry C. Boyte, *Everyday Politics: Reconnecting Citizens and Public Life* (Philadelphia: University of Pennsylvania Press, 2004); John P. Kretzmann and John L. McKnight, *Building Communities from the Inside Out: A Path toward Finding and Mobilizing a Community's Assets* (Chicago: ACTA, 1993).
7. See Albert W. Dzur, *Punishment, Participatory Democracy, and the Jury* (New York: Oxford University Press, 2012) for more on load-bearing participation.
8. Alexis de Tocqueville, *Democracy in America*, ed. Olivier Zunz, trans. Arthur Goldhammer (New York: The Library of America, 2004), pp. 585–587.
9. John Dewey, *The Public and Its Problems*, in *John Dewey, The Later Works: 1925–1953*, vol. 2, ed. J. A. Boydston (Carbondale: Southern Illinois University Press, 1981), p. 327.
10. Tony Judt has poignantly illustrated this displacement in brief personal sketches of the lost civic world of his British childhood. See *The Memory Chalet* (New York: Penguin, 2010).
11. Zygmunt Bauman, "Ethics of Individuals," *Canadian Journal of Sociology* 25 (2000): 86.
12. Ibid., p. 87.
13. In Nils Christie, *A Suitable Amount of Crime* (New York: Routledge, 2004), pp. 4–6. I put his narrative in my own words, but the essentials are the same.
14. Ibid., pp. 69–70.
15. Sheldon S. Wolin, "Norm and Form: The Constitutionalizing of Democracy," in *Athenian Political Thought and the Reconstruction of American Democracy*, ed. J. Peter Euben, John R. Wallach, and Josiah Ober (Ithaca, NY: Cornell University

Press, 1994), p. 36. See also Wolin, *Politics and Vision: Continuity and Innovation in Western Political Thought, Expanded Edition* (Princeton, NJ: Princeton University Press, 2004), pp. 601–603.

16. Wolin, "Fugitive Democracy," pp. 18–19.

17. Wolin, *Democracy Incorporated: Managed Democracy and the Specter of Inverted Totalitarianism* (Princeton, NJ: Princeton University Press, 2008), pp. 255, 277.

18. Wolin, *Democracy Incorporated*, p. 277.

19. Wolin, *Politics and Vision, Expanded Edition*, p. 603. See Harry C. Boyte, *The Backyard Revolution: Understanding the New Citizen Movement* (Philadelphia: Temple University Press, 1980).

20. Wolin, "Fugitive Democracy," p. 23.

21. Wendy Brown, "American Nightmare: Neoliberalism, Neoconservatism, and De-democratization," *Political Theory* 34 (2006): 692. See also Brown, *Undoing the Demos: Neoliberalism's Stealth Revolution* (New York: Zone Books, 2015).

22. Wendy Brown, "Neo-liberalism and the End of Liberal Democracy," *Theory & Event* 7 (2003): Section 9.

23. Ibid.

24. Brown, "American Nightmare," p. 694.

25. Ibid., p. 703.

26. Ibid., p. 704.

27. Ibid., p. 705.

28. Archon Fung, "Recipes for Public Spheres: Eight Institutional Design Choices and Their Consequences," *Journal of Political Philosophy* 11 (2003): 338–339.

29. Ibid.

30. James S. Fishkin, *When the People Speak: Deliberative Democracy and Public Consultation* (New York: Oxford University Press, 2009), p. 59.

31. Note, though, that some scholars have identified some possible sources of negative influence. Matthew Flinders, for example, argues mini-publics mistakenly raise community expectations for government accountability and transparency they cannot deliver upon, thus increasing rather than decreasing dysfunctional citizen distrust of government and politicians. See, e.g., "Daring to Be a Daniel: The Pathology of Politicized Accountability in a Monitory Democracy," *Administration & Society* 43 (2011): 595–619. Yannis Papadopoulos argues that the increase in public forums outside government has distracted attention from the increase in technocratic elite decision making behind the scenes. See "On the Embeddedness of Deliberative Systems: Why Elitist Innovations Matter More," in *Deliberative Systems*, ed. John Parkinson and Jane Mansbridge (Cambridge: Cambridge University Press, 2012), pp. 125–150.

32. See Mark B. Brown, "Survey Article: Citizen Panels and the Concept of Representation," *The Journal of Political Philosophy* 14 (2006): 208.

33. John Dryzek, *Foundations and Frontiers of Deliberative Governance* (New York: Oxford University Press, 2008), p. 168.

34. For more on this point, see Dzur, *Punishment, Participatory Democracy, and the Jury* (New York: Oxford University Press, 2012), ch. 5, "Juries, Juries, Everywhere, But Not Inside the Courts."

35. Pierre Rosanvallon, *Counter-Democracy: Politics in an Age of Distrust* (Cambridge: Cambridge University Press, 2008), p. 33.

36. Ibid., p. 52.

37. Ibid., p. 55.

38. http://www.oregon.gov/circ/Pages/Initiative-Review.aspx.

39. Rosanvallon, *Counter-Democracy*, p. 121.

40. Ibid, p. 191.

41. Ibid.

42. Henrik Paul Bang and Signe Kjaer Jorgensen, "Political Authority as Genuineness— How to Transgress New Public Spheres," *Northern Lights* 7 (2009): 83.

43. Ibid., p. 86.

44. Ibid.

45. Henrik P. Bang, "Everyday Makers and Expert Citizens: Building Political not Social Capital," ANU working paper, p. 26.

46. Henrik Bang, "Among Everyday Makers and Expert Citizens," in *Remaking Governance: Peoples, Politics and the Public Sphere*, ed. Janet Newman (Bristol: Policy Press, 2005), p. 165.

47. Ibid.

48. Ibid., p. 166.

49. Ibid., p. 167.

50. Ibid.

51. Ibid., p. 168.

52. Ibid, p. 169.

53. Bang, "Everyday Makers and Expert Citizens," p. 8.

54. Ibid., p. 19.

55. Weber, *Economy and Society*, ed. G. Roth and C. Wittich (Berkeley: University of California Press, 1978).

56. "Alignment occurs when gears mesh," writes Mathews, "when institutions and citizens work in a complementary, mutually reinforcing fashion. The work citizens do puts control in their hands, and it also benefits institutions. Institutions become more effective as they profit from the work of citizens. And they are likely to become more responsive when they see the benefits from this work." Mathews, *The Ecology of Democracy*, p. 140.

57. Ibid., p. 142.

58. See James P. Levine, *Juries and Politics* (Belmont, CA: Wadsworth, 1992), p. 95. As Justice Stevens puts this point, "Voting for a political candidate who vows to be 'tough on crime' differs vastly from voting at the conclusion of an actual trial to condemn a specific individual to death." Harris v. Alabama, 513 U.S. 504, 518 (1995) (Stevens, J., dissenting).

59. See John Doble, "Attitudes to Punishment in the US—Punitive and Liberal Opinions," in *Changing Attitudes to Punishment*, ed. J. Roberts and M. Hough (Portland, OR: Willan, 2002), pp. 148–162. Julian Roberts calls the moderation of punitive attitudes after closer proximity to a specific offender "one of the most robust and often-replicated findings" in the field of criminal justice research. Roberts, "The Future of State Punishment," in *Retributivism Has a Past: Has It a Future?*, ed. M. Tonry (New York: Oxford University Press, 2011), p. 105.

60. Marc Stears has also called for more collaboration in workplaces and in public life. I share his goals, but disagree when he posits "relationships" as primary levers of change. I think we have found it hard enough to maintain decent— much less friendly—civic relationships across race, class, and education divisions. Collaborative work in public places can result in a sobering-up process, however, that calls our attention to other people not like us. Civic relationships can emerge, of course, but I think civic sobriety is a demanding-enough goal. See Stears, *Everyday Democracy: Taking Centre-Left Politics beyond State and Market* (London: Institute for Public Policy Research, 2011).

CHAPTER 2

1. See the discussion in Peter Levine, *We Are the Ones We Have Been Waiting For* (New York: Oxford University Press, 2013).

2. Jeremy Waldron offers a salient general critique of contemporary political theory— not just pessimists and proceduralists—for neglecting institutions in his "Political Political Theory: An Oxford Inaugural Lecture," *New York University School of Law: Public Law and Legal Theory Research Series*, Working Paper No. 12-26 (2011).

3. Robert Bellah, R. Madsen, W. M. Sullivan, A. Swidler, and S. M. Tipton, *The Good Society* (New York: Knopf, 1991), p. 291.

4. Ibid., p. 256.

5. Ibid., p. 273.

6. "The function of institutions is always the same," writes Talcott Parsons, a pioneer in this field—"the regulation of action in such a way as to keep it in relative conformity with the ultimate common values and value-attitudes of the community." Parsons, "Prolegomena to a Theory of Social Institutions," *American Sociological Review* 55 (1990): 331.

7. "To institutionalize," writes Philip Selznick, "is to infuse with value beyond the technical requirements of the task at hand." Selznick, *The Moral Commonwealth: Social Theory and the Promise of Community* (Berkeley: University of California Press, 1992), p. 233.

8. Robert Michels, *Political Parties: A Sociological Study of the Oligarchical Tendencies of Modern Democracy* (Glencoe: Free Press, 1962), p. 365.

9. See Ricardo Blaug, *How Power Corrupts: Cognition and Democracy in Organisations* (London: Macmillan, 2010). Blaug convincingly argues that conventional treatments

of organizations in Michels and elsewhere have mistakenly naturalized hierarchy and have failed to capture its destabilizing and nonfunctional characteristics.

10. Mary Douglas, *How Institutions Think* (Syracuse: Syracuse University Press, 1986), p. 99.

11. Ibid., p. 92.

12. Ibid., p. 102.

13. Zygmunt Bauman, *Modernity and the Holocaust* (London: Polity, 1989), p. 199.

14. Ibid., p. 103.

15. Ibid., p. 195.

16. Erving Goffman, *Asylums: Essays on the Social Situation of Mental Patients and Other Inmates* (Chicago: Aldine, 1962).

17. See, e.g., D. G. Burnett, *A Trial by Jury* (New York: Vintage, 2001) on jury service as bureaucratic and disempowering, but note that Gastil et al. found jurors more likely to have a positive civic experience when they deliberate more, when the case they are adjudicating is complex—the more of a load they are expected to bear—and when they are treated well by court professionals. John E. Gastil, P. Deess, P. J. Weiser, and C. Simmons, *The Jury and Democracy: How Jury Deliberation Promotes Civic Engagement and Political Participation* (New York: Oxford University Press, 2010).

18. Lucia Zedner, "Reflections on Criminal Justice as a Social Institution," in *The Eternal Recurrence of Crime and Control: Essays in Honour of Paul Rock*, ed. D. Downes, D. Hobbs, and T. Newburn (London: Oxford University Press, 2010), p. 71.

19. Ibid., p. 72.

20. William J. Stuntz, *The Collapse of American Criminal Justice* (Cambridge, MA: Harvard University Press, 2011), p. 255.

21. See Nils Christie, "Conflicts as Property," *The British Journal of Criminology* 17 (1977): 2; and Howard Zehr, *Changing Lenses: A New Focus for Criminal Justice*, (Scottdale, PA: Herald Press, 1990), p. 121.

22. The "vast majority of crime problems" are handled through "social policy and social institutions beyond the criminal process." Nicola Lacey, "Social Policy, Civil Society and the Institutions of Criminal Justice," *Australian Journal of Legal Philosophy* 26 (2001): 9. As Zedner puts it, "to assume that crime control is the prerogative of criminal justice agents and institutions obscures the role played in controlling crime by informal sources and institutions of social order—not least the family, the school, religious institutions, and the community. Such ability as criminal justice institutions have to tackle crime relies heavily upon these informal sources of order and their interdependent relationship with them." "Reflections on Criminal Justice as a Social Institution," p. 73.

23. National Public Radio, "States Release Inmates Early to Cut Prison Costs," *Weekend Edition Sunday*, December 13, 2009.

24. See Jeremy Waldron, "The Core of the Case against Judicial Review," *The Yale Law Journal* 115 (2006): 1345–1406.

25. Nils Christie, *A Suitable Amount of Crime* (New York: Routledge, 2004), p. 114.

26. It is commonplace for intellectual histories of democratic theory to view participatory theory as a kind of primitive first draft or first stage of more sophisticated deliberative democratic theory. For a more nuanced account, see Antonio Floridia, *From Participation to Deliberation: A Critical Genealogy of Deliberative Democracy* (Colchester, UK: ECPR Press, 2017).

27. See, e.g., Carole Pateman, "Participatory Democracy Revisited," *Perspectives on Politics* 10 (2012): 7–19; Francesca Polletta, "Participatory Democracy in the New Millennium," *Contemporary Sociology* 42 (2013): 40–50; and Donatella della Porta, *Can Democracy Be Saved?* (Malden, MA: Polity Press, 2013).

28. See della Porta, *Can Democracy Be Saved?*, p. 173.

29. See, e.g., Maryland Farmer, Letter IV, in *The Complete Anti-Federalist*, vol. 5, ed. Herbert J. Storing (Chicago: University of Chicago Press, 1981), p. 38; Federal Farmer, Letter IV, in *The Complete Anti-Federalist*, vol. 2, pp. 249–50.

30. See Peter Laslett's classic discussion of participatory democracy as best suited for a simpler, "face to face" society. "Face to Face Society," in *Philosophy, Politics and Society*, First Series, ed. Peter Laslett (New York: Macmillan, 1956), pp. 157–184.

31. Arnold Kaufman, "Human Nature and Participatory Democracy," in *Responsibility*: NOMOS III., ed. Carl J. Friedrich (New York: Liberal Arts Press, 1960), p. 192

32. Ibid., p. 184.

33. Students for a Democratic Society, "The Port Huron Statement" (1962), http://www.lsa.umich.edu/phs/resources/porthuronstatementfulltext.

34. Kaufman, "Human Nature and Participatory Democracy," p. 189.

35. Ibid.

36. Students for a Democratic Society, "The Port Huron Statement."

37. Breton, "The Ideology of the Person," *New University Thought* 2 (1962): 11.

38. Straughton Lynd, "The New Radicals and 'Participatory Democracy'" *Dissent* 12 (Summer 1965): 324.

39. Meta Mendel-Reyes, *Reclaiming Democracy: The Sixties in Politics and Memory* (New York: Routledge, 1995). See also Marc Stears, *Demanding Democracy: American Radicals in Search of a New Politics* (Princeton, NJ: Princeton University Press, 2010).

40. As criminologist and democratic innovator Clifford Shearing has noted, many police departments in the United States and elsewhere resist power-sharing because they see social order as their professional responsibility. See Albert Dzur, "Conversations on Restorative Justice: A Talk with Clifford Shearing," *Restorative Justice* 4(3): 410–423.

41. I borrow the word from Pat Carlen, who uses the word "responsibilize" critically and ironically in her critique of contemporary criminal justice. See, e.g., *A Criminological Imagination: Essays on Justice, Punishment, Discourse* (New York: Routledge, 2016).

CHAPTER 3

1. In her study of seven principals of democratic schools, Edith A. Rusch comments, "they are educators whose stories are seldom found in texts about leading schools." "Many silenced voices began to emerge, thus creating opportunity for the reframing of knowledge and action in school communities and university curriculum and instruction." "Leadership in Evolving Democratic School Communities," *Journal of School Leadership* 8 (May) 1998: 244. Indeed, many of the democratic professional administrators she interviewed noted they had to "unlearn" top-down administrative instruction they received early in their careers.

2. Dana Mitra and Steven Jay Gross, "Increasing Student Voice in High School Reform: Building Partnerships, Improving Outcomes," *Educational Management Administration & Leadership* 37 (2009): 523.

3. Dana Mitra, "Student Voice in School Reform: Reframing Student-Teacher Relationships," *McGill Journal of Education* 38 (2003): 302.

4. Interview. See also Albert W. Dzur, "Trench Democracy in Schools #3: An Interview with Vanessa Gray," *Boston Review* (July 11, 2014), (http://www.bostonreview.net/blog/albert-w-dzur-trench-democracy-schools-3-vanessa-gray). Accessed May 30, 2018.

5. Deborah Meier, "What's Democracy Got to Do with Teaching," *Kappa Delta Pi Record* (Fall, 2011): 19

6. Deborah Meier, *The Power of Their Ideas: Lessons for America from a Small School in Harlem* (Boston: Beacon Press, 2002) (2nd edition), p. 124.

7. Deborah Meier, "Our Democracy Is Weak Now, Let's Fight for It in Schools," "Bridging Differences" blog entry, *Education Week* (March 23, 2017).

8. See https://www.facebook.com/NationalLeagueOfDemocraticSchoolsnlds/ and https://www.scasd.org/Page/4528. Accessed May 30, 2018.

9. See http://democraticeducation.org/index.php/about-us. Accessed May 30, 2018.

10. This word reverberates in democratic professional reform narratives: "[P]eople only burn out when they're treated like appliances," says Deborah Meier, *Power of Their Ideas*, p. 149.

11. Dianne C. Suiter, "Finding Our Voice: One School's Commitment to Community," *Journal of Educational Controversy* 3 (2008): 3.

12. Harry C. Boyte and Margaret J. Finders, "'A Liberation of Powers': Agency and Education for Democracy," *Educational Theory* 66 (1–2) (2016): 136.

13. Paul McCormick, *Leadership in a Democratic School.* Unpublished dissertation, Penn State University, 2017, p. 3.

14. Quoted in Jim Strickland, "The Real Source of Our Education Crisis" (League of Democratic Schools essay on file with author).

15. Michael W. Apple and James A. Beane (eds.), *Democratic Schools: Lessons in Powerful Education,* 2nd ed. (Portsmouth, NH: Heinemann, 2007), p. 20. This

well-regarded and oft-cited practitioner casebook is made up of essays written by democratic teachers and principals about their schools.

16. Deborah Meier, *In Schools We Trust: Creating Communities of Learning in an Era of Testing and Standardization* (Boston: Beacon Press, 2002), p. 2.

17. Ibid., 12.

18. Nelson Beaudoin, *Elevating Student Voice: How to Enhance Student Participation, Citizenship and Leadership* (Larchmont, NY: Eye On Education, Inc., 2005), p. 12.

19. Dana L. Mitra, "The Significance of Students: Can Increasing 'Student Voice' in Schools Lead to Gains in Youth Development?" *Teachers College Record* 106 (2004): 651–688.

20. Interview.

21. Apple and Beane, *Democratic Schools*, p. 86.

22. George H. Wood, "Teaching for Democracy," *Educational Leadership* (November 1990): 37.

23. Meier, *In Schools We Trust*, p. 177.

24. Apple and Beane, *Democratic Schools*, p. 13.

25. Vale D. Hartley, "The Elementary Classroom: A Key Dimension of a Child's Democratic World," *Journal of Educational Controversy* 3 (2008): 7.

26. Jim Strickland and Dianne Suiter, "Toward Democratic Schools," in *Education and the Making of a Democratic People*, ed. John Goodlad, Roger Soder, and Bonnie McDaniel (Boulder, CO: Paradigm, 2008), p. 127.

27. Meier, *Power of Their Ideas*, p. 8.

28. Ibid., p. 7.

29. Wood, "Teaching for Democracy," p. 34. This student was attending Central Park East school.

30. Meier, "What's Democracy Got to Do with Teaching," p. 20.

31. Dana Mitra and Stephanie C. Serriere, *Civic Education in the Elementary Grades: Promoting Student Engagement in an Era of Accountability* (New York: Teachers College Press, 2015), p. 5.

32. Interview.

33. Democracy can easily turn into forms that are "citizen lite"—"a democracy with citizens and civic work on the margins." Mathews, *Ecology of Democracy*, p. 66.

34. Apple and Beane, *Democratic Schools*, p. 17.

35. Ibid., pp. 17–18.

36. This narrative was written by Kerry Salazar, a 1st grade teacher at Opal School in Portland, Oregon and published in *The Opal* (Winter 2011): 2.

37. Meier, *Power of Their Ideas*, pp. 1–2.

38. Ibid., p. 2.

39. McCormick, *Leadership in a Democratic School*, p. 78.

40. Ibid., p. 74.

41. As Meier puts this point, "Only if schools are run as places of reflective experimentation can we teach both children and their teachers simultaneously. . . . Schools

must create a passion for learning not only among the children but also among their teachers." *Power of Their Ideas*, p. 140.

42. Apple and Beane, *Democratic Schools*, p. 43. Visitors to democratic schools often make such observations: cross-generational activities and collaborations encourage greater responsibility among adolescents who are working alongside "little kids."

43. Deborah Meier, "So, What Does It Take to Build a Democratic School?" *Phi Delta Kappan* 85 (2003): 19.

44. Interview.

45. Dianne C. Suiter, "Finding Our Voice: One School's Commitment to Community," *Journal of Educational Controversy* 3 (2008): 5.

46. Beaudoin, *Elevating Student Voice*, p. 85.

47. Interview. See also Albert W. Dzur, "Trench Democracy in Schools: An Interview with Principal Donnan Stoicovy," *Boston Review* (Nov 8, 2013) (http://bostonreview.net/blog-us/albert-w-dzur-trench-democracy-schools-interview-principal-donnan-stoicovy). Accessed May 30, 2018.

48. Interview. See "Westside Village Magnet School Family Handbook 2012–13," pp. 18–20.

49. Deborah Meier underscores this point in "So, What Does It Take to Build a Democratic School?" and elsewhere.

50. Strickland and Suiter, "Finding Our Voice," p. 135.

51. This story draws from interviews and from the article, "Young Citizens Take Action for Better School Lunches," by Stephanie Serriere, Dana Mitra, and Jennifer Cody, *Social Studies and the Young Learner* 23 (2010): 4–8.

52. Reflecting on his visits to democratic schools across the country, Wood expresses a sentiment that matches my own experience: "The moment you step into these schools, you know something special is going on. The first clues are visual. It might be that the halls are full of student projects and art work. Or the absence of posted rules carefully spelling out what one can or cannot do. Or brightly painted murals where one would usually see drab, industrial-strength-green cinder block." He continues, "Then notice the kids. Moments after you enter the school, they want you to know this is a special place. One child takes you by the hand to show you her painting on the wall. Another offers to read to you from his journal." "Teaching for Democracy," pp. 34–35. As Theresa Perry puts it, "there are things about a school that tell you whom it belongs to from the moment you walk into the lobby." Quoted by Deborah Meier, *In Schools We Trust*, p. 91.

53. Suiter, "Finding Our Voice," p. 6.

54. Meier, "So, What Does It Take to Build a Democratic School?," p. 6.

55. McCormick, *Leadership in a Democratic School*, p. 98.

56. Interview.

57. Dana Mitra, Stephanie Serriere, Donnan Stoicovy, "The Role of Leaders in Enabling Student Voice," *Management in Education* 26 (2012): 107.

58. Interview. See also, Cristina Alfaro, "Reinventing Teacher Education: The Role of Deliberative Pedagogy in the K-6 Classroom," in *Deliberation and the Work of Higher Education*, ed. John R. Dedrick, Laura Grattan, and Harris Dienstfrey (Dayton, OH: Kettering Foundation Press, 2008), pp. 143–164.

59. Meier, *Power of Their Ideas*, p. 14.

60. Interview. See http://www.ithacacityschools.org/lacs. Accessed May 30, 2018.

61. Interview. See, https://www.scasd.org/Page/4504. Accessed May 30, 2018.

62. Interview.

63. YATST was founded by democratic educator Helen Beattie. See Albert W. Dzur, "Trench Democracy in Schools #2: An Interview with Helen Beattie," *Boston Review* (Feb 14, 2014) (http://bostonreview.net/blog/albert-w-dzur-trench-democracy-schools-2-interview-helen-beattie). Accessed May 30, 2018.

64. YATST, "Re-Imagine Learning," (Fall Newsletter, 2012).

65. Interview.

66. This is a suggestion Joe Greenberg made during our interview, namely, that there be a way of accrediting democratic teachers, providing those who had spent time in democratic schools a certificate in collaborative education.

67. In her study comparing three student voice efforts in the Bay Area, Mitra found the longest lasting program enjoyed the support of a community-based organization. Interview. See also Mitra, "Student Voice from the Inside and Outside: The Positioning of Challengers," *International Journal of Leadership in Education: Theory and Practice* 9 (2006): 322–326.

68. YATST is one program facilitated by the organization UP for learning dedicated to increasing student voice and co-ownership of education: http://www.upforlearning.org/. Accessed May 30, 2018.

69. Helen Beattie asserts that "We prefer to be a coach on the side as things evolve, diminishing the level of support/coaching over time as the schools capacity builds—but not needing to leave as a means for 'program legitimacy.'" Interview.

CHAPTER 4

1. See Robert Martinson's report, "What Works? Questions and Answers about Prison Reform," *The Public Interest* 35 (1974): 22–54.

2. See Loic Wacquant, "Class, Race and Hyperincarceration in Revanchist America." *Daedalus* (Summer, 2010): 74–90.

3. William J. Stuntz, *The Collapse of American Criminal Justice* (Cambridge, MA: Harvard University Press, 2011), p. 33.

4. Heather C. West and William J. Sabol, "Prisoners in 2007," *Bureau of Justice Statistics Bulletin* (December 2008). https://www.bjs.gov/content/pub/pdf/p07.pdf. While still greatly outpacing all other peer countries, the US prison population has declined over the last eight years, with 1.5 million inmates now behind bars. See E. Ann Carson and Elisabeth Anderson, "Prisoners in 2015," *Bureau of Justice*

Statistics Bulletin (December 2016), https://www.bjs.gov/content/pub/pdf/p15.pdf.

5. Lauren E. Glaze and Thomas P. Bonczar, "Probation and Parole in the United States, 2007 Statistical Tables," Bureau of Justice Statistics (December 2008), http://www.justicestudies.com/pubs/livelink8-1.pdf. The most recent data show little change in the numbers of Americans under correctional supervision, with 4.6 million people under community supervision, probation, or parole in 2015. See Danielle Kaeble and Thomas P. Bonczar, "Probation and Parole in the United States, 2015," *Bureau of Justice Statistics Bulletin* (December 2016), https://www.bjs.gov/content/pub/pdf/ppus15.pdf.

6. Marc Mauer, *Race to Incarcerate*, 2nd ed. (New York: The New Press, 2006), p. 95.

7. See Marie Gottschalk, *The Prison and the Gallows: The Politics of Mass Incarceration in America* (Cambridge: Cambridge University Press, 2006) and "Dollars, Sense, and Penal Reform: Social Movements and the Future of the Carceral State," *Social Research* 74 (2007): 669–694. The rural prison economy is especially relevant here. See Rebecca Thorpe, "Democratic Politics in an Age of Mass Incarceration," in *Democratic Theory and Mass Incarceration*, ed. A.W. Dzur, I. Loader, and R. Sparks (New York: Oxford University Press, 2016), pp. 18–32.

8. See, e.g., Nicola Lacey, "American Imprisonment in Comparative Perspective," *Daedalus* (Summer 2010): 102–114.

9. "Children whose parents are imprisoned are likely to experience feelings of shame, humiliation, and loss of social status," writes Mauer. "They begin to act out in school or distrust authority figures. . . . In far too many cases, these children come to represent the next generation of offenders." *Race to Incarcerate*, p. 204.

10. See Jeff Manza and Christopher Uggen, *Locked Out: Felon Disenfranchisement and American Democracy* (New York: Oxford University Press, 2005).

11. Bruce Western and Becky Pettit, "Incarceration and Social Inequality," *Daedalus* (Summer 2010): 13.

12. The class dimensions of these data are borne out by the fact that "the lifetime chance of serving time for African American men with some college education *decreased* from 6 percent to 5 percent" over the same period. Wacquant, "Class, Race and Hyperincarceration," p. 79.

13. Dorothy E. Roberts, "The Social and Moral Costs of Mass Incarceration in African American Communities," *Stanford Law Review* 56 (2004): 1272.

14. Eric Holder, "Remarks at the Annual Meeting of the American Bar Association's House of Delegates" (San Francisco, August 12, 2013). http://www.justice.gov/opa/speech/attorney-general-eric-holder-delivers-remarks-annual-meeting-american-bar-associations.

15. Jay Caspian Kang, "Our Demand Is Simple: Stop Killing Us," *New York Times Magazine* (May 4, 2015).

16. Keeanga-Yamahtta Taylor, *From #BlackLivesMatter to Black Liberation* (Chicago: Haymarket Books, 2016), p. 14.

17. Eric Lichtblau and Jess Bidgood, "Baltimore Agrees to Broad Change for Troubled Police Dept," *New York Times* (January 12, 2017). The decree involves reforms such as greater transparency and increased community oversight.

18. Taylor, *From #BlackLivesMatter*, p. 174.

19. Ibid, p. 189.

20. For an overview, see, e.g., David W. Van Ness and Karen Heetderks Strong, *Restorative Justice: An Introduction to Restorative Justice*, 4th ed. (New Providence: Matthew Bender & Company, 2010).

21. While these states have the highest numbers of restorative justice programs, many other states are experimenting with a few small-scale programs. See Gordon Bazemore and Mara Schiff, *Juvenile Justice Reform and Restorative Justice: Building Theory and Policy from Practice* (Devon, UK: Willan, 2005), p. 105. Restorative justice language is present in a majority of state statutes and codes, though accompanied by a wide array of mandates and funding—some more robust than others. See Sandra Pavelka, "Restorative Justice in the States: An Analysis of Statutory Legislation and Policy," *Justice Policy Journal* 13 (2) (2016): 1–23.

22. See Dzur, *Democratic Professionalism*, ch. 6, and "Restorative Justice and Democracy: Fostering Public Accountability for Criminal Justice," *Contemporary Justice Review* 14 (2011): 367–381.

23. See Franklin E. Zimring, Gordon Hawkins, and Sam Kamin, *Punishment and Democracy: Three Strikes and You're Out in California* (Oxford: Oxford University Press, 2001).

24. Nils Christie, "Conflicts as Property," *The British Journal of Criminology* 17 (1977): 1–15; Howard Zehr, *Changing Lenses: A New Focus for Criminal Justice* (Scottdale, PA: Herald Press, 1990); John Braithwaite, *Restorative Justice and Responsive Regulation* (New York: Oxford University Press, 2002).

25. See Bernard E. Harcourt, "The Invisibility of the Prison in Democratic Theory: A Problem of 'Virtual Democracy'" *The Good Society* 23 (2014): 6–16.

26. See Robert P. Burns, *The Death of the American Trial* (Chicago: University of Chicago Press, 2009).

27. For more on this topic, see Dzur, *Punishment, Participatory Democracy, and the Jury*.

28. See Dzur, *Democratic Professionalism*, ch. 6, and David Karp "Harm and Repair: Observing Restorative Justice in Vermont," *Justice Quarterly* 18 (2001): 727–757.

29. http://doc.vermont.gov/justice/restorative-justice/. Accessed May 30, 2018.

30. See Lauren Abramson and D. B. Moore, "Transforming Conflict in the Inner City: Community Conferencing in Baltimore," *Contemporary Justice Review* 4 (2001): 321–340.

31. https://www.restorativeresponse.org/conferencing/ Accessed May 30, 2018.

32. Interview with Lauren Abramson. See also Albert W. Dzur, "Trench Democracy in Criminal Justice #1: An Interview with Lauren Abramson," *Boston Review* (Dec

13, 2013) (http://www.bostonreview.net/blog/albert-w-dzur-trench-democracy-criminal-justice-interview-lauren-abramson). Accessed May 30, 2018.

33. Ibid.

34. Ibid.

35. Ibid.

36. Ibid.

37. See Albert Dzur, "Conversations on Restorative Justice: A Talk with Kay Pranis," *Restorative Justice*, 4 (2) (2016): 261.

38. Interview with Sugatha Baliga, founder of Community Works, Oakland.

39. https://www.washingtonpost.com/graphics/national/police-shootings-2016. Accessed May 30, 2018.

40. Patrick Healy and Jonathan Martin, "His Tone Dark, Donald Trump Takes G.O.P. Mantle," *New York Times* (July 21, 2016).

41. https://www.whitehouse.gov/briefings-statements/the-inaugural-address/. Accessed May 30, 2018.

42. David Alan Sklansky, "Police and Democracy," *Michigan Law Review* 103 (7) (2005): 1779.

43. Wesley Skogan, *Police and Community in Chicago: A Tale of Three Cities* (New York: Oxford University Press, 2006), p. 142.

44. Anthony C. Thompson, "It Takes a Community to Prosecute," *Notre Dame Law Review* 77 (2002): 321–372.

45. On community policing as a democratic innovation, see Archon Fung, "Putting the Public Back into Governance: The Challenges of Citizen Participation and Its Future," *Public Administration Review* 75 (4) (2015): 517, and *Empowered Participation: Reinventing Urban Democracy* (Princeton, NJ: Princeton University Press, 2004).

46. Tom R. Tyler, "From Harm Reduction to Community Engagement: Redefining the Goals of American Policing in the Twenty-First Century," *Northwestern University Law Review* 111 (6) (2017): 1552–1553.

47. Sklansky, "Police and Democracy," p. 1798.

48. See Albert Dzur, "Conversations on Restorative Justice: A Talk with Clifford Shearing," *Restorative Justice* 4 (3) (2016): 410–423.

49. John Dewey, *Democracy and Education* [1916], in *John Dewey, The Middle Works: 1899–1924*, vol. 9, ed. J. A. Boydston (Carbondale: Southern Illinois University Press, 1980), p. 368.

50. Vivian Gussin Paley, *You Can't Say You Can't Play* (Cambridge, MA: Harvard University Press, 1992).

51. The middle schoolers were coached by University of Minnesota undergraduates involved in the Center for Democracy and Citizenship's Public Achievement program, which is motivated by ideas of citizen agency and more democratic forms of professionalism. See Harry C. Boyte, *Everyday Politics: Reconnecting Citizens and Public Life* (Philadelphia: University of Pennsylvania Press, 2004).

52. This story is based on an interview with Vanessa Gray. See also Albert W. Dzur, "Trench Democracy in Schools #3: An Interview with Vanessa Gray," *Boston Review* (July 11, 2014) (http://www.bostonreview.net/blog/albert-w-dzur-trench-democracy-schools-3-vanessa-gray). Accessed May 30, 2018.

53. See http://www.insideoutcenter.org/network.html. Accessed May 30, 2018.

54. For a description of the program by its founder, see Lori Pompa, "One Brick at a Time: The Power and Possibility of Dialogue across the Prison Wall," *The Prison Journal* 93 (2) (2013): 127–134.

55. Interview with Lisa Guenther. See also Albert W. Dzur, "Teaching Philosophy on Death Row: An Interview with Lisa Guenther," *Boston Review* (June 26, 2015) (http://www.bostonreview.net/blog/dzur-trench-democracy-1). Accessed May 30, 2018. Guenther's discussion group is strictly voluntary and is not a credit-bearing course affiliated with a university.

56. Ibid.

57. Interview with Max Kenner. See also Albert W. Dzur, "Trench Democracy in Criminal Justice #3: An Interview with Max Kenner," *Boston Review* (Dec 11, 2014) (http://bostonreview.net/blog/albert-w-dzur-trench-democracy-criminal-justice-3-interview-max-kenner). Accessed May 30, 2018.

58. Interview with William DiMascio. See also Albert W. Dzur, "Trench Democracy in Criminal Justice #2: An Interview with William DiMascio," *Boston Review* (May 16, 2014) (http://www.bostonreview.net/blog/albert-w-dzur-trench-democracy-criminal-justice-2-interview-william-dimascio). Accessed May 30, 2018.

59. Ibid.

60. Ibid.

61. Civic organization among current inmates themselves is another avenue. Though it has traditionally been thwarted by legal decisions upholding prison administration directives regarding inmate safety, there is evidence that inmate-led prison councils lead to less violent prison conditions. See Amy E. Lerman and Vesla Mae Weaver, "A Trade-Off between Safety and Democracy? An Empirical Investigation of Prison Violence and Inmate Self-Governance," in *Democratic Theory and Mass Incarceration*, ed. A. W. Dzur, I. Loader, and R. Sparks (New York: Oxford University Press, 2016), pp. 238–265.

62. On the possibility of bipartisan coalition building, see Carl Hulse, "Unlikely Cause Unites the Left and the Right: Justice Reform," *New York Times* (Feb. 18, 2015).

63. Margaret Urban Walker, *Moral Understandings: A Feminist Study in Ethics*, 2nd ed. (New York: Oxford University Press, 2007).

64. http://sustainabilityinprisons.org/about/. Accessed May 30, 2018.

65. Roger Jarjoura, *Indiana's Juvenile Reentry Program: Aftercare for Indiana through Mentoring* (AIM) (Indianapolis: Aftercare for Indiana through Mentoring, 2005).

CHAPTER 5

1. "Thousands of direct public engagement processes are conducted across the United States each year, the majority of which occur at the local level in counties, cities, towns, villages, and municipal authorities." Tina Nabatchi and Lisa Blomgren Amsler, "Direct Public Engagement in Local Government," *American Review of Public Administration* 44 (2014): 69. Interestingly, scholars and practitioners have difficulty naming what is happening and use more than a dozen different terms— such as "engagement," "collaboration," and "deliberation"—when they talk about the new ways public administrators are working with citizens. I suspect it is not the novelty or the multiplicity of the forms that make them hard to name, but the fact that in many cases the democratic possibilities are in tension with a persistent managerial imperative.

2. Woodrow Wilson, "The Study of Administration," *Political Science Quarterly* 2 (1887): 217.

3. Larkin S. Dudley and Ricardo S. Morse, "Learning about Deliberative Democracy in Public Affairs Programs," in *Deliberation and the Work of Higher Education: Innovations for the Classroom, the Campus, and the Community*, ed. John Dedrick, Harris Dienstfrey, and Laura Grattan (Dayton, OH: Kettering Foundation Press, 2008), pp. 165–190.

4. Interview with Larkin Dudley.

5. Matt Leighninger, "Teaching Democracy in Public Administration: Trends and Future Prospects," in *The Future of Public Administration around the World*, ed. Rosemary O'Leary, David M. Van Slyke and Soonhee Kim (Washington DC, Georgetown University Press, 2010), p. 238.

6. Valerie A. Lemmie, *Democracy beyond the Ballot Box: A New Role for Elected Officials, City Managers, and Citizens* (Dayton, OH: Kettering Foundation Press, 2008), pp. 5 and 7.

7. Tina Nabatchi, "Addressing the Citizenship and Democratic Deficits: The Potential of Deliberative Democracy for Public Administration," *The American Review of Public Administration* 40 (2010): 381.

8. Interview with Ricardo Morse.

9. Valerie Lemmie's career spanned this transformative period of neoliberalism and new government reforms: "As a practicing city manager, the literature I read and the professional development training I attended focused almost exclusively on managing city government more like a business, establishing performance measurements and creating an environment for competitive service delivery and treating citizens like customers." *Democracy beyond the Ballot Box*, p. 14.

10. Mark Bevir, *A Theory of Governance* (Berkeley: University of California Press, 2013), p. 9.

11. Ibid., p. 151.

12. Ibid., p. 196.

13. Archon Fung, "Varieties of Participation in Complex Governance," *Public Administration Review* (2006) (December: Special Issue on Collaborative Public Management): 74.

14. Ibid., p. 67.

15. Lemmie, *Democracy beyond the Ballot Box* , p. 8.

16. Ibid, p. 14.

17. On the concept of "wicked problems," see Horst W. J. Rittel and Melvin M. Webber, "Dilemmas in a General Theory of Planning," *Policy Sciences* 4 (2) (1973): 155–169.

18. Lemmie, *Democracy beyond the Ballot Box*, p. 31.

19. Interview with Chris Plein.

20. Interview with Jamie Verbrugge. See also Albert W. Dzur, "Trench Democracy in Public Administration #3: An Interview with Jamie Verbrugge," *Boston Review* (Oct 10, 2014). http://bostonreview.net/blog/albert-dzur-trench-democracy-jamie-verbrugge. Accessed May 30, 2018.

21. Ibid.

22. Lemmie, *Democracy beyond the Ballot Box*, p. 55.

23. Interview with Kimball Payne. See also Albert W. Dzur, "Trench Democracy in Public Administration: An Interview with Kimball Payne," *Boston Review* (Jan 17, 2014). http://bostonreview.net/blog/dzur-trench-democracy-public-administration-interview-kimball-payne. Accessed May 30, 2018.

24. See, e.g., Peter Levine, *We Are the Ones We Have Been Waiting For: The Promise of Civic Renewal in America* (New York: Oxford, 2013), pp. 94–95.

25. As Lemmie moved along in her career she began to realize that her managerialism fed into the public disengagement she was trying to redress: "I did not yet understand," she says about her early days in the profession, "that I, too, was part of the problem. There are structural, institutional, and organic reasons for the disconnect between citizens and their government, and one of them, going back over a century, was the advent of the 'professional' or 'expert' in local government, in the form of the city manager. For too long we have assumed that improving government efficiency, like building a better car, was the answer." *Democracy beyond the Ballot Box*, p. 9.

26. Interview with Andrea Arnold. See also Albert W. Dzur, "Trench Democracy in Public Administration #2: An Interview with Andrea Arnold," *Boston Review* (March 21, 2014), http://bostonreview.net/blog/albert-w-dzur-trench-democracy-public-administration-2-interview-andrea-arnold. Accessed May 30, 2018.

27. Tina Nabatchi, "Why Public Administration Should Take Deliberative Democracy Seriously," in *The Future of Public Administration around the World*, ed. Rosemary O'Leary, David M. Van Slyke, and Soonhee Kim (Washington DC: Georgetown University Press, 2010), p. 163.

28. Interview with Kim Payne.

29. Ibid.

30. Editorial, "Talking with Each Other for a Brighter Future," *Lynchburg News & Advance* (January 13, 2008).

31. Interview with Kim Payne.

32. Ibid.

33. As democratic city manager Mary Bunting of Hampton, Virginia relates, "We didn't expect people to come just to us. We went to them. . . . We went to the soccer clubs, and the PTA meeting, and the Girls and Boys Scouts, anywhere anybody would take us. We set up a booth at the YMCA and the local town center." Michael McGrath, "Hampton, Virginia: Civic Engagement as a Management Strategy," *National Civic Review* (Winter 2015): 31.

34. Interview with Kim Payne.

35. Ibid.

36. Ibid.

37. Michael McGrath, "Decatur, Georgia: Diversity, Gentrification, and the Art of Community Conversation," *National Civic Review* (Summer 2016): 25–33..

38. "On Our Way: 2010 Strategic Plan, City of Decatur, Georgia" http://www.decaturga.com/about/master-plans/2010-strategic-plan.

39. Interview with Andrea Arnold.

40. Ibid.

41. Ibid.

42. Ibid.

43. Ibid.

44. Ibid.

45. Ibid.

46. Ricardo Morse, "Citizens Academies: Local Governments Building Capacity for Citizen Engagement," *Public Performance & Management Review* 36 (2012): 79–101.

47. McGrath, "Hampton, Virginia: Civic Engagement as a Management Strategy," 29.

48. In his North Carolina study, Morse found that "many programs may be missing the full potential of these programs" by focusing "primarily on public relations." He reports that "it is the outliers that stand out" in terms of substantive civic agency. "Citizens Academies," p. 96.

49. On the development of participatory budgeting in Porto Alegre, see Boaventura de Sousa Santos, "Participatory Budgeting in Porto Alegre: Toward a Redistributive Politics," *Politics and Society* 26 (1998): 461–508.

50. See http://www.pbchicago.org/pb-in-chicago.html and https://www.participatory-budgeting.org/. Accessed May 30, 2018.

51. This discussion of Chicago's 49th Ward draws from Josh Lerner's narrative in *Everyone Counts: Could "Participatory Budgeting" Change Democracy?* (Ithaca, NY: Cornell University Press, 2014), pp. 11–14. Lerner's nonprofit organization, the Participatory Budgeting Project, assisted Alderman Moore throughout the initial process.

52. Moore explained, "anger and mistrust aren't healthy for democracy. We need a new governance model, one that empowers people to make real decisions about policy and spending decisions." Joe Moore, "Spending Out in the Open for 49th Ward," *Chicago Tribune* (March 31, 2010).

53. As one reporter notes, "The greatest value of participatory budgeting has been as a means of access to local stewardship and government more generally by those . . . who have otherwise felt disenfranchised or denied." Ginia Bellafante, "Participatory Budgeting Opens Up Voting to the Disenfranchised and Denied," *New York Times* (April 17, 2015).

54. Lerner, *Everyone Counts*, p. 31.

55. "Throughout the process, there was argument and debate, some heated and some healthy. But that is exactly what . . . participants said was the most positive part. Agencies and politicians aside, strangers found a way to work together and commit to honoring one another's priorities, while considering the good of their neighborhoods. And that ultimately was the point." Soni Sangha, "Putting in Their 2 Cents," *New York Times* (March 30, 2012).

56. Lerner, *Everyone Counts*, p. 38.

57. Lerner, *Everyone Counts*, p. 31.

58. While the demands can be burdensome, they are also experienced as developmentally valuable. "In some cases, young people voluntarily spent months researching community needs using census and other data, visiting the sites of proposed projects, navigating municipal budgets and mastering technical funding criteria. When interviewed, they told us they'd gained leadership and research experience along the way—developing skills such as public speaking, creating legible poster boards that presented proposals to their communities at large, facilitating difficult conversations and chairing meetings." Celina Su, "What Makes Young People More Excited about Politics? Deciding How to Spend Municipal Budgets," *Washington Post* (October 17, 2016).

59. Anne Li, "This Is What Democracy Looks Like: Participatory Budgeting Begins in Chicago for 2016," *South Side Weekly* (January 25, 2016).

60. Interview with Kim Payne.

61. Interview with Jamie Verbrugge.

62. Aaron Leavy, "Fort Collins, Colorado: An Expectation of Public Engagement," *National Civic Review* (Spring 2016): 52.

63. Lemmie, *Democracy beyond the Ballot Box*, p. 47.

64. Interview with Valerie Lemmie.

65. Interview with Kim Payne.

CHAPTER 6

1. Interview with Vanessa Gray.

2. George Wood, *Time to Learn*, p. xxii.

3. "Hermeneutics of suspicion" is a phrase associated with Paul Ricoeur, who used it in some of his work to characterize the skeptical strands in the theories of Freud, Marx, and Nietzsche, which sought to "unmask" conventional nineteenth century beliefs about self, society, economics, and politics. See, e.g., *Freud and Philosophy* (Yale University Press, 1970). I borrow it to draw attention to the way scholars are approaching participatory democratic innovations with an eye on "unmasking" conventionally uncritical attitudes about their overall value.

4. See, e.g., Tina Nabatchi and Matt Leighninger, *Public Participation for 21st Century Democracy* (New York: Jossey-Bass, 2015).

5. Archon Fung, "Continuous Institutional Innovation and the Pragmatic Conception of Democracy," *Polity* 44 (2012): 609–624.

6. See Wendy Brown, *Undoing the Demos: Neoliberalism's Stealth Revolution* (New York: Zone, 2015) and Colin Crouch, *Post-Democracy* (Malden, MA: Polity Press, 2004).

7. Isaac William Martin, "The Fiscal Sociology of Public Consultation," in *Democratizing Inequalities: Dilemmas of the New Public Participation*, ed. Caroline Lee, Michael McQuarrie, and Edward T. Walker (New York: NYU Press, 2015), pp. 103, 119.

8. See Michael McQuarrie, "Community Organizations in the Foreclosure Crisis: The Failure of Neoliberal Civil Society," *Politics & Society* 4 (2012): 73–101 and "No Contest: Participatory Technologies and the Transformation of Urban Authority," *Public Culture* 25 (2013): 143–175.

9. Edward T. Walker, "Legitimating the Corporation through Public Participation," in *Democratizing Inequalities: Dilemmas of the New Public Participation*, p. 66.

10. Caroline Lee, *Do-It-Yourself Democracy* (New York: Oxford University Press, 2015), pp. 150–151.

11. Ibid., p. 155.

12. McQuarrie, "No Contest," pp. 169, 145.

13. Nina Eliasoph, *The Politics of Volunteering* (Malden, MA: Polity, 2013), p. 134.

14. Lee, *Do-It-Yourself Democracy*, p. 221.

15. Eliasoph, *Politics of Volunteering*, p. 152.

16. Lee, *Do-It-Yourself Democracy*, p. 95.

17. Ibid, pp. 127–128, 201.

18. McQuarrie, "Community Organizations" and "No Contest."

19. Lee, *Do-It-Yourself Democracy*, p. 161. See also Nina Eliasoph, *Making Volunteers: Civic Life after Welfare's End* (Princeton, NJ: Princeton University Press, 2011).

20. McQuarrie, "Community Organizations," pp. 80–84.

21. Lee, *Do-It-Yourself Democracy*, p. 221; cf. Eliasoph, *Politics of Volunteering*, p. 126.

22. Eliasoph, *Politics of Volunteering*, p. 87.

23. Lee, *Do-It-Yourself Democracy*, p. 27, ital. in original.

24. On the priority of racial justice over democracy, see Dorothy E. Roberts, "Democratizing Criminal Law as an Abolitionist Project," *Northwestern University Law Review* 111 (6) (2017): 1597–1608. On abolitionism as the proper expression of democratic commitments, see Peter Ramsay, "A Democratic Theory of Imprisonment," in *Democratic Theory and Mass Incarceration*, ed. A. W. Dzur, I. Loader, and R. Sparks (New York: Oxford University Press, 2016), pp. 84–113.

25. McQuarrie, "No Contest," p. 147.

26. Walker, "Legitimating the Corporation," p. 77.

27. Ibid.

28. Eliasoph, *Politics of Volunteering*, p. 122.

29. Ibid, p. 87.

30. See, e.g., Theda Skocpol, *Diminished Democracy: From Membership to Management in American Civic Life* (Norman: University of Oklahoma Press, 2003).

31. Lee, for example, draws a stark contrast between social movement activity, which she sees as having a chance at real world efficacy, and participatory innovations such as deliberative forums, which do not: "Just as empowerment through self-discipline is fostered in youth organizations, in deliberative dialogue on youth issues, social action is channeled toward community-oriented cultural change, not mobilization targeting national actors. Whether it is designed to spark activism or explicitly intended to produce consent, public engagement has surprisingly consistent effects, focusing action on 'strength-based' approaches at the individual or local level, while authority and coordinated advocacy at larger scales is ceded to elite sponsors and organizations." Lee, *Do-It-Yourself Democracy*, pp. 167, 226.

32. See Harry C. Boyte, *Everyday Politics: Reconnecting Citizens and Public Life.* Philadelphia: University of Pennsylvania Press (2004); Henrik P. Bang, "Everyday Makers and Expert Citizens: Building Political Not Social Capital," ANU working paper; Peter Levine, *We Are the Ones We Have Been Waiting For* (New York: Oxford University Press, 2013).

33. For this criticism, see Peter Levine, "Saving Relational Politics," *Perspectives on Politics* 14 (2016) (2): 468–473.

34. Eliasoph, *Politics of Volunteering*, pp. 121–122.

35. Francesca Polletta, "Public Deliberation and Contention," in *Democratizing Inequalities: Dilemmas of the New Public Participation*, p. 236. See also Polletta, "Just Talk: Public Deliberation after 9/11," *Journal of Public Deliberation* 4 (2008).

36. Polletta, "Public Deliberation and Contention," pp. 238–239.

37. Pierre Rosanvallon, *Counter-Democracy: Politics in an Age of Distrust* (Cambridge: Cambridge University Press, 2008).

38. Mick McKeown, "Re-imagining Professionalism while Thinking About a New Politics of Mental Health," Economic and Social Research Council Workshop on Re-Imagining Professionalism in Mental Health: Towards Co-Production (2016), https://coproductionblog.wordpress.com/.

39. Pamela Fisher, "Co-production: What Is It and Where Do We Begin?," *Journal of Psychiatric and Mental Health Nursing* 23 (2016): 345.
40. Sarah Carr, "On No More Throwaway People," ESRC Workshop on Re-Imagining Professionalism in Mental Health: Towards Co-Production (2016), https://coproductionblog.wordpress.com/.
41. Ibid.
42. Pamela Fisher, "Overview," ESRC Workshop on Re-Imagining Professionalism in Mental Health: Towards Co-Production (2016), https://coproductionblog.wordpress.com/.
43. Ibid.
44. Gemma Stacey and Philip Houghton, "An Imperfect Model for Democratic Decision Making," ESRC Workshop on Re-Imagining Professionalism in Mental Health: Towards Co-Production (2016), https://coproductionblog.wordpress.com/.
45. Tina Coldham, "Co-Production Shouldn't Be on Lonely Street," ESRC Workshop on Re-Imagining Professionalism in Mental Health: Towards Co-Production (2016), https://coproductionblog.wordpress.com/.
46. Interview with Pamela Fisher.

CONCLUSION

1. See, e.g., *Democracy's Education: Public Work, Citizenship, and the Future of Colleges and Universities*, ed. H. C. Boyte (Nashville, TN: Vanderbilt University Press, 2014).
2. Dewey, "Education as Politics" (1922). In *John Dewey: The Middle Works, 1899–1924*, vol. 13, ed. J. A. Boydston (Carbondale: Southern Illinois University Press, 1986).
3. Interview with Helen Beattie.
4. Zygmunt Bauman, *Legislators and Interpreters: On Modernity, Post-Modernity and Intellectuals* (Ithaca: Cornell University Press, 1987).
5. As Sanford Schram puts it, "The focus of such research would be on citizens as subjects for action, rather than objects of inquiry." Schram, "Citizen-Centered Research for Civic Studies: Bottom Up, Problem Driven, Mixed Methods, Interdisciplinary," in *Civic Studies: Approaches to the Emerging Field*, ed. Peter Levine and Karol Sołtan (Washington, DC: Bringing Theory to Practice, 2014), pp. 91–102.

Index